LIFE'S WORK

Confessions of an

Unbalanced Mom

LISA

BELKIN

SIMON & SCHUSTER

New York   London   Toronto   Sydney

SIMON & SCHUSTER
Rockefeller Center
1230 Avenue of the Americas
New York, NY 10020

First Simon & Schuster trade paperback edition 2003

SIMON & SCHUSTER and colophon are registered trademarks
of Simon & Schuster, Inc.

For information about special discounts for bulk purchases,
please contact Simon & Schuster Special Sales:
1-800-456-6798 or business@simonandschuster.com

Designed by Katy Riegel

Manufactured in the United States of America

3   5   7   9   10   8   6   4   2

The Library of Congress has cataloged the Simon & Schuster
hardcover edition as follows:
Belkin, Lisa
Life's work : confessions of an unbalanced mom / Lisa Belkin.
p.   cm.
1. Belkin, Lisa, date.   2. Working mothers—United States—Biography.
3. Women journalists—United States—Biography.   4. Work and
family—United States.   I. Title.
HQ759.48   .B45 2002
306.874'3'092—dc21
[B]   2002018778

ISBN 0-7432-2541-4
0-7432-2543-0 (Pbk)

To the thousands who on 9/11
gave their lives at work

CONTENTS

CONTENTS

CONTENTS

INTRODUCTION

I used to think that life was linear. A straight line, from A to Z, mailroom to CEO, the first day of work to the gold retirement watch. You decide what you want to be and then you make a beeline in that direction. Simple.

I also used to think that life could be "balanced"—a word that I have come to hate. It sounds like some sort of tantric yoga position, a contorted pose that others on the mat can do because they are *really* trying. As you might have guessed, I'm not very good at yoga.

This book is the story of how I gave up on straight lines; how I learned to zig and zag, to leapfrog and jump backward. It's also the story of how I gave up on balance and decided to settle for a close approximation of sanity, instead. (Disclaimer: I have not actually attained sanity yet, but am ever hopeful.)

There was a time when I didn't think about any of this. I was single in Manhattan back then, a brand-new reporter at the newspaper of every reporter's dreams. I spent all available moments at the office without feeling that I was giving up any part of my life. This job *was* my life. Then I met Bruce, and the office didn't seem quite as interesting anymore. A doctor-in-training, he was moving to Houston months after we met to complete a four-year fellowship program. I knew nothing about Houston, except that it was hot and I hate the heat. In a decision that was anything but logical or linear I quit my dream job at *The New York Times,* married a man I'd known for less than a year, and moved to Texas.

New city. No job. A new husband who not only worked all day, but sometimes all night. The best way to meet new people, I'd learned, was to interview them, so I began freelancing for the newspaper I'd just quit and stumbled into the best professional experience of my life. I discovered that I was jazzed by a kind of work I had never had a chance to try—dashing around the state, using Southwest Airlines as though it were a taxi service, hopscotching from one story to the next. I learned I had a knack for longer, more thoughtful writing, too. I wrote some of my first magazine articles while in Texas, and my first book.

But the most important things I learned didn't become clear until I had returned to New York, to a full-time job in the newsroom, with my husband and three-month-old child in tow. The first lesson Texas taught me was that editors don't have to see you in order to edit you. I had answered copy desk questions from pay phones from Lubbock to Brownsville, and it made no difference where I was. This was back in the dark ages, when cell phones were the size of those crank-up models used in the Korean War and only a few show-offs carried them around. But I insisted on one and smugly sat on the train each evening at six instead of seven, answering questions from the copy desk in a rolling extension of the office.

When I became pregnant with my second son three years later, I decided to leave the paper completely. It was a decision that made as little sense as my decision to move to Houston, but one that made me just as proud of myself. Look at me, I crowed silently. Aren't I just the essence of modern motherhood? I'll freelance from home. I'll write another book. I'll nurse my newborn with one hand and type an article with the other hand, all while a nutritious family dinner simmers on the stove.

I certainly used both my hands. The problem was, I needed four or five more. I had changed the location of my juggling act, but not the juggling itself. Here are just a few of the highlights, seared forever into my memory:

- My first day as a work-at-home-mom. I pulled on my sweats (which was, after all, the point of this entire plan) and shuffled downstairs for breakfast with my son. Then I kissed him sweetly on the top of his head, handed him to his baby-sitter, and said brightly, "Mommy is going upstairs to work now." That's when he began to wail. He shrieked outside my office door for the better part of two days, not understanding why Mommy was *home* but was not *his*. On the third morning, I pulled on my panty hose and a suit, kissed him again, then drove to the nearby diner for a cup of coffee and a muffin. After about an hour, I snuck back into my own house and went to work.
- The frantic morning when the baby-sitter was sick, and we were at a crucial potty-training moment. So I

moved the boy, the potty, and the job-well-done stickers into my office, where my interviews with Very Important Sources were periodically interrupted by squeals of "Mommy, I have to pee."

- The afternoon of the yearly doctor checkup, this one a visit requiring *shots*. I had promised I would be there—what is the point of working at home if you can't make it to the visits that include *shots*?—but it turned out that a magazine story I'd written was closing at exactly the same time as the doctor's appointment. So I sat on a chair in the waiting room, my nervous little boy's head on my lap, and the magazine galleys draped over him as I scribbled changes, then phoned them in to the copy desk.

Since I am such a healthy example of balance, the editors of the *Times* asked me to write a column. We called it Life's Work, and what you are about to read includes many of the columns I think say it best, along with lots of new material about what I learned while writing all those columns. Think of the columns as the pineapple, and the whole of my life story as the Jell-O. I've kept each chapter short because, if you're like me, there's only time enough to read a few pages between sliding into bed and collapsing into sleep.

My editors say Life's Work is about the intersection of life and work. I say it is about the collisions that happen daily at that intersection. Either way, the subject appealed to the many parts of my fractured self. The reporter in me understood that this emotional and economic tug-of-war is the central story of our generation. And the conflicted parent in me—the one who thought working from home would be the solution but found it only created different problems— saw a chance to get advice. I envisioned Life's Work as a kaleidoscope of voices, sometimes mine, often strangers I met along the way. It would be an ongoing conversation on the page, and maybe it would offer me some answers. So please feel free to talk back to the book. That's part of the point.

We reporters always believe we will change the world through our work, when the truth is our work inevitably changes *us*. My first columns reflected my life; soon they began to shape my life. I did find answers—surprisingly simple answers—but they were not at all what I'd expected they'd be. In part they came from noticing truths and shadows in my world that had been there all along: the intricate legacy of work, for instance, that my family had passed down through the generations and which was an unseen hand behind choices I'd thought were uniquely my own.

Most of the answers, though, came from listening. My E-mail address ran with every column, and over time I heard from thousands of readers—women and men, married and single, parents and nonparents. There were notes from a couple of newlywed workaholics who were determined to make time in their day to meet each other for lunch. There were letters from a CEO father-to-be who was trying to re-structure his entire company so he would have time to see his baby. There was a cry for help from the divorced mom who thought she might have to give away the family iguana because the store that sold live food closed before she got home from work. (Their stories are all in here; read on.) Yet in all that electronic conversation, over all this time, one letter never arrived. I have yet to hear from *anyone* who feels they are doing everything right.

So it's not just me who can't do this—and it's not just you, either. Not a one of us seems to be able to give 100 percent of themselves to their job *and* 100 percent of themselves to their family *and* 100 percent of themselves to taking care of themselves. Small wonder. Yet we all seem to think someone (else) out there is getting it right; people who work full-time think people who work part-time are doing it, and people who work part-time think people who don't work at all are doing it, and those who left the office to tend to home think that if only they could escape back to an office, they might find sanity. But all of this misses the point. No one can do it, because it cannot be done.

Read that last sentence again. *It cannot be done.* This book you are holding, filled with the tales of my life and the lives of all those strangers, is crystallized around that simple thought. It cannot be done. So let's start forgiving ourselves when we can't do it.

On the day of the pivotal doctor-visit-with-shots, I looked up from my galleys, my cell phone, and my whimpering son and saw a woman on the other side of the waiting room glaring at me. I wanted to march over and say, "At least I'm *here,* aren't I?" But I stayed put and tried something I had never done before. I simply shrugged. This was not a metaphorical shrug, but a physical one. And it felt good.

Go ahead. Shrug. Lift those shoulders. Breathe deep. Raise your hands in mock surrender toward the ceiling and repeat after me: "So what?"

So what if the house isn't as clean as it could be?

So what if that last business report was not the best you have ever written?

So what if you're eating takeout for the second night in a row, or haven't been to the gym in weeks, or sent your children to school in crumpled shirts on school picture day?

So what if you have to answer questions from the copy desk while at the doctor's office?

I am not saying that none of these things matter. They all matter, but not all the time. I am as bad at math as I am at yoga, but even I know that 100 percent plus 100 percent plus 100 percent equals more than any one person can do in a day.

So what?

LOVE

(AND WORK)

AND MARRIAGE

WORK ETHIC

I was about seven years old when I stood at the bus stop with a playmate and cheerfully wove an elaborate tale of woe. "I have to sew all the costumes for the class play," I chirped. "*And* finish the script, *and* memorize the songs, *and* do fifty pages of math homework and one hundred words of spelling." Had I heard of *War and Peace* back then, I would have thrown that in, too. "I might not even go to sleep," I crowed. "I might have to work all night."

No, of course I didn't need to do any of those things, but my tendency to inflate the truth when I was seven is not the point here. The point is what I chose to inflate. While other kids were exaggerating how far they could throw a ball or how many Barbies they owned, I was boasting about work. The forty-year-old me is both amused and appalled at the fact that the seven-year-old me chose being overworked as a measure of my worth. I remember feeling puffed with importance as I spun my tale, certain that the harder you worked and the more time you spent at it, the better you must be.

Where the heck did I get this idea? More to the point, have I gotten over it yet? We'll deal with that second question later, but the answer to the first is that I suspect this was a mutation of what my parents were actually trying to teach me: that work had value, that it made you feel whole, that a seven-year-old who was hopeless at throwing a ball and who was not allowed to own a Barbie could find an identity as a thinker and a creator.

I was taught all of this against the backdrop of Long Island in the 1960s, a cookie-cutter place filled with children of the city who had grown up and vowed not to raise their own children there. They'd moved out to the suburbs in order to relax. Then they spent exhausting hours each day commuting back to the city they had fled. My father found a way out of this paradox. He was an orthodontist and worked from a suite of offices in what would otherwise have been the garage of our split-level house. He took every Friday off, saw patients half the day on Saturday, and ate lunch nearly every afternoon with other dentists at the local diner. My father loved his work and would spend long, almost leisurely hours fiddling with the plaster molds of a patient's teeth as if it were more hobby than career.

My mother, on the other hand, was happy only when she was charging forward. Some women my age struggle against the memory of a mother always there with home-baked cookies. Mine never baked anything (we teased that she should just convert the oven into bookshelves), and my early memories are a blur of business suits and Crock-Pot meals as she leapfrogged through a series of professions, trying to find one that could keep up with her. If she had been born a few generations later she could have been president, but her timing was such that she became commander in chief of all our lives. For birthdays and graduations she would send my cousins checks with cards that read: "May you have everything you are willing to work for." A morning person to the extreme, she caught the 6:03 train into the city every morning. While fellow passengers napped, she completed *The New York Times* crossword puzzle, in ink.

"Why can't you be like a normal mother?" I would ask, muttering something about cookies. Not that I had any interest in cookies, but I knew with a child's unerring instinct that this made her feel guilty and that her guilt worked well for me. While I was layering on the guilt, however, I was also taking mental notes, as if I knew that this whirring life was my destiny, too.

I sensed from the start that my mother didn't work like this because she had to, but because she loved to. It was a work ethic arrived at honestly, perhaps genetically, passed down to her from those who came before, as tangible as any family heirloom. Her own father was a Russian immigrant who managed to accumulate a B.S., an M.B.A., and two years of medical school before he ran out of money. He became a jeweler, then spent his life encouraging everyone around him to go to graduate school. He begged my mother to get a law degree at a time when that simply wasn't done, and he was heartbroken when she decided to follow in my grandmother's footsteps and become a teacher instead.

Grandma was another one who did not believe in doing one thing when two would do. She taught third grade for nearly fifty years and was the kind of demanding but life-changing teacher parents dream of for their kids. (She never cooked, either, although it took me a long time to figure that out. I always loved her chicken matzo ball soup. Not until I was in my twenties did I realize that it came from the deli on West Seventy-second Street, making me the only girl in New York City who could order her grandmother's chicken soup via takeout.) When Grandma finally retired, she took up traveling with the same passion she had poured into teaching. In her seventies she went to Cambodia. She visited Beijing before Nixon, and, because she was kosher, she lugged cans of tuna along. A week before she died, at the age of eighty-seven, she signed up for a two-year series of courses in the history of China at a local university.

And then there's her sister. My firecracker of a great-aunt kept the books for a series of businesses for many decades. She retired in her late seventies. Ten years later she ran into a casting director during a morning at the Laundromat. The next thing she knew she was an actress in TV commercials. She loved the chauffeured cars and the dressing rooms, and she especially loved the bragging rights. "Working," she said, shortly before her hundredth birthday last year, "is better than not working."

I could obviously sing that tune as early as age seven. But what I didn't see back then is that all these hard chargers took breaks from their work. My grandmother walked almost everywhere, and she would soak up the world as she went. My great-aunt loved betting on the horses and writing schmaltzy poems. Even my mother, the most frenetic of the three, would put down her newspaper on the morning train and knit her way into Penn Station. By the time I was seven I had polished the work-as-life ethic to a high gloss. I spent the next thirty years learning to slow down.

FOR LOVE OR MONEY

During the years of my childhood, our household menagerie included two cats, a bird, many, many fish, and three dogs, one of them an oversized Airedale named Barney who was big enough to ride. Because of this—and because of too many hours spent reading *Doctor Doolittle*—I announced early in life that I would be a veterinarian when I grew up. This delusion lasted into high school, when I realized that vets were actually doctors, and doctors needed to pass chemistry.

I retrenched and decided I would become a lawyer instead. It would have made my grandfather proud. My college essays described how I might mesh my love of foreign language with my high school debating skills for a career in international law. I can admit now that I was never sure what exactly an international lawyer does and that all languages sound like Greek to me. When I flunked the Spanish placement quiz during the first week of college (then flunked it again after a full year of college Spanish), I gave up on that plan, too.

I did not give up on law entirely, though. I dutifully applied to law school during my senior year, but not out of any blinding passion. I applied because I had no idea what I wanted to be when I grew up, and law seemed a good credential for something more interesting when it finally came along.

My college years had been spent flirting with another road, however. Journalism. Although I never thought of it as a career choice, I somehow found myself at the school newspaper, or radio station, or writing workshops so regularly that I should have realized this was something more than a passing crush. I found time for just one application for a newspaper job while slaving over my dozen or more applications to law school. Come graduation, I had an acceptance letter to the University of Virginia School of Law in one hand and an offer to answer the phones and deliver mail at *The New York Times* in the other.

I sent a hundred-dollar deposit to Charlottesville, then asked for a one-year deferral. I spent that year in the Washington bureau of *The New York Times,* falling in love. I suspected that my parents were worried that I would never make a living chasing this particular dream, but there's no stopping passion. My job title during my first year was "clerk," which meant I was a gofer eight hours a day, but the other sixteen were mine to write articles, which the editors would agree to look at. I am still introduced by one of those editors as "the worst clerk the metro desk ever had." It's a charitable description. Lost in my own world of interviews, I would ignore the phones and the filing.

After what would have been my first year of law school, I received a computer glitch of a letter from U. Va. saying that

I owed it one hundred dollars, and if I did not pay, I would not be allowed to register for the second year. After what would have been my second year, I received the same letter saying I could not register for the third year, and, right on schedule a year later, the letter said I must pay one hundred dollars or forfeit my diploma. By then I had elbowed my way into a job as a reporter at the *Times* (I think they promoted me to clear a spot for someone who would actually answer the phones), and if journalism salaries had been as high as legal salaries, I would have sent the hundred dollars just to see what happened next.

As slowly as I fell in love with work, that's how quickly I fell in love with Bruce. We met on a blind date (he was actually a last-minute substitute for someone else) on a bitingly cold December night. For the first three hours I wasn't interested. He was about to move to Houston, so what was the point? But he laughed at most of my jokes, and he had a passion for life that I suspected might bring out the best in me. We talked about work on that first date, and there is nothing quite as sexy as a man who cares for children for a living, even (especially?) to someone like me, who wasn't sure she could handle the messy, unpredictable, unknown world of kids. We were engaged four months after we met, and we were married seven months after that.

Fact is, we never would have gotten married that quickly if not for work. Our decision went something like this: Bruce was about to leave on a springtime trip to Houston to find a place to live when he moved there permanently come July. In the days before his trip, I was summoning the courage to ask the *Times* for a transfer to the Houston bureau so I could, eventually, join him.

"It just doesn't sound professional," I fretted, "to say 'there's this *really* nice guy and he's moving to Texas, so could I move there, too? Pretty please?' "

"Would it sound more professional to say that that nice guy was your fiancé?" Bruce asked, startling us both.

It's not the proposal I'd dreamed of since childhood, and it's certainly nothing that Bruce had planned, but it was right for us.

The irony, of course, is that although I became engaged as a bow to work, I soon left work because I was engaged. The powers-that-be didn't seem to think they needed another reporter in the Houston bureau, even if her fiancé was *really* nice. So I quit. Like my decision not to go to law school, this really wasn't a decision at all, but a response to some gravitational pull.

Looking back, it was also the first clash between my life and my work. I chose my life—but not hands down. I had turned away from law without a glance backward; my newspaper job was harder to let go. I developed a most annoying verbal tic—the need to tell people that although now I was just a freelancer, I used to work full-time for *The New York Times*. I tucked my *Times* ID card into a corner of my purse and carried it with me for four years in Texas, until all that remained was a faded shred.

COMPETITION

Truth be told, there was another reason I became a writer—a reason that had nothing to do with law school or *The New York Times,* and everything to do with a guy. This particular guy was the editor of the college newspaper, and he was the reason I walked into a newsroom for the very first time. We combined love and work at that newspaper for nearly two years, and while he taught me volumes about writing, I also learned a lesson he didn't mean to teach. The day he was chosen for *The Washington Post* internship and I was not, was the day I realized I could never marry him. He did nothing so boorish as gloat; in fact, he barely dared to celebrate, but I ended things anyway. I'm not proud of this fact, but I knew even then that I am too competitive (and too insecure?) to go through life with someone who does the same work that I do.

This quirk became one of the first things I wrote about when I became a workplace columnist, and I soon learned that the economy might cease to function if everyone felt the way I did. "Where else do you meet people?" asked Fran

Rodgers, one of the many experts to take me under her wing. Fran was the founder of WFD, a Boston consulting company specializing in employee loyalty. (Not coincidentally, her husband is her company's second-in-command.) People spend more of their time at work, she said, and women are doing jobs once done mostly by men. The result? Corporate courtship. One of Fran's clients found that 30 percent of employees who went through that company's training program married a fellow employee. Add to that the spate of entrepreneurial start-ups, many begun by couples who work out of their homes, and you have a chunk of the workforce sharing work while sharing life—navigating the territory that I ran away from all those years ago.

When I talked to them, they started with the advantages. "We're *both* creating the marriage and we're *both* creating the business," said Jeff Multz of his wife, Susan, whom he met because she was a client of his computer consulting business in Atlanta. After they married, she became the president of the company and he, as vice president of sales and marketing, reported to her.

Even spouses who were not growing a business described a sense of partnership. "We speak the same language," said Linda Safran, who happens to be a favorite relative of mine by marriage. She's the head of the department of Greek and Latin at Catholic University of America in Washington and her husband, Adam Cohen, is a medieval art historian. That fact came in handy when she was ordered to bed during a complicated pregnancy, and he stepped in at the last moment and taught all her courses for three months.

But these couples also confirmed my fear that work-love mergers can cause headaches. When Susan Multz first joined her husband's company, she recalled, "Every week I was grabbing my keys and quitting." Why? "Because," her husband answered dryly, "I was the president and she wasn't." Instead of calling a marriage counselor, they brought in a management consultant, who suggested that Susan take on the day-to-day operations of the company—and the title of president.

No amount of consulting or counseling, however, can solve Adam and Linda's problem. There are only four slots for medieval art professors in all of Washington, and because all four are filled at the moment (one of those by Linda), Adam has been unable to find a job. Moving is not really an option—how many universities would be able to hire two arcane specialists at the same time? So Adam stays home, where he writes manuscripts, cares for their son, Josiah, and wonders if he should give up on his field altogether.

The last time we spoke about this he still said that he did not resent his wife as she leaves each day to do the work he is also trained to do. "I'm angry all the time," he said, "but never at Linda." As I've already confessed, I don't think I could be as selfless as all that. I'd be more like a dear friend of mine, a screenwriter out in California, whose husband landed his dream job as a staff writer for a hit TV show. Unfortunately, it is also *her* dream job, and she didn't take it well.

"Sure, I'm happy for him," she said morosely. "But then I have to go back to my little office to write my pathetic little scripts." She found herself reminding people, loudly and often, that, at age thirty-five, she was much, much younger than her forty-something husband. In other words, he had a head start.

My own forty-something husband and I have a different sort of buffering distance between us. Bruce is a pediatric heart specialist who runs a genetic research lab, and when he writes, it is in a language I can only pretend to understand. (He asked me to proofread a paper of his when we were first married, and check for run-on sentences. "These are run-on *words*," I wailed on page two, and he hasn't bothered to ask since.)

Yes, sometimes I miss the easy shorthand of couples who do the same things, but I'm pleased to trade that for the complete absence of competition. I am freed to be the best writer in the house, just as he is the best doctor. The fact that he will never scoop me on a story is hardly the reason I married this remarkable man. But it sure is a relief to know that he won't.

BY ANY OTHER NAME

Belkin is the name I was born with. It means "squirrel" in Russian, and my great-grandfather carried it with him to America when he fled the tsar. Gelb is my husband's name. It means "yellow" in German, and Bruce's great-grandfather brought it out of Hungary, allowing it to live on in defiance of Hitler. On our application for a marriage license I declared that my legal name would be Lisa Belkin Gelb, linguistically turning myself into a yellow squirrel. This was my way of navigating the rocky questions of identity and commitment, independence and tradition that modern marriage brings. What it doesn't say on that paper is that I planned to be Lisa Belkin at work and Lisa Gelb at home—a tidy division of two worlds which, I've since learned, cannot be tidily divided.

"What's in a name?" Shakespeare asked, arguing that roses are roses and that names make no difference. Easy for him to say. He killed off Juliet so quickly that she never had to decide whether to keep her "maiden" name (an archaic term if ever there was one), or take her husband's name, or hyphenate for the sake of the children. She didn't have to warn each successive temp at her office switchboard that the school nurse might call and ask for someone not in the voice-mail directory. She never had to pause before signing a credit card slip, wondering which of two signatures to use. She never had to argue with airport security because the name on her passport (her "married name") didn't match the name on her ticket (her "work name"). And she never had to stand at the dry cleaner or the video store and sound like a computer hacker looking for the magic password: "Capulet. Or maybe it's under Montague. If that doesn't work, try Capulet Montague—no hyphen."

I do all these things. They are the complicated side effects of a simple decision. There was no question that I would keep my name when I got married, because my byline was hard-won and without it I would seem to disappear. (A colleague of mine at the *Times* wrote an article the day she returned from her honeymoon, then walked around the office polling everyone she could find about whether to change her byline. When, after much agonizing, she finally decided to add her married name to her existing name, she was told by her editors that the combination had one too many letters to fit.)

There was also no question that very modern me wanted the very old-fashioned symbolism of sharing a last name with my husband and, eventually, my children (who, by the way, each have Belkin as their middle name; no hyphen). As a friend of mine said of his decision to take his *wife's* name after marriage: "If you play on the same team, you should wear the same uniform."

So now I change my uniform dozens of times every day,

taking fleeting mental measure of who I am and what I am about every time I introduce myself. Does this person know me from home or from work? Am I at this meeting because I am a writer or a mother? My two selves even have separate personalities. Lisa Belkin talks faster and is bubblier at parties. She's taller, too, probably because she stands up straighter and wears heels more often. Lisa Gelb is partial to T-shirts, black leggings, and dangly earrings. She chews gum too much and she likes to cook. In a crowded room, she's more likely to listen than to talk.

At first I felt as if the "work" me was the real me and the other me was just pretend. I couldn't introduce my married self with a straight face, and when the hygienist at the dentist's office came into the waiting room asking for Mrs. Gelb, I would look around for my mother-in-law. Over the years, though, I've grown into the part. Now Lisa Gelb is the person I mellow into when I'm finished being professional for the day. More important, it is a reminder that there is (or, at least, there should be) a relaxed, closed-for-business-until-tomorrow side of me. The chance to burrow into my alter ego makes it worth the confusion caused by having one in the first place.

At a school event not long ago I was talking with a woman I had known since both of our ten-year-old sons were in preschool. She happened to mention a magazine article she'd read. It was an article I had written, although she had no way of knowing that because she knew me only by my married name.

"You're Lisa *Belkin?*" she asked when I confessed.

"That's me," I answered, "but only some of the time."

LUNCH

Meet Brandon and Jill Lowitz, two giddy Manhattan newly-weds, who, when they first wrote to me, were immersed in their work but wanting to spend more time with each other. She was in marketing for a fashion designer; he was in business development for an Internet start-up. "We get out of work, then I go to the gym, she goes to yoga," Brandon said. "By the time we get home it's eight-thirty, eight-forty-five, and you're so tired that lively conversation isn't even possible."

Their "together time" was crammed into the weekends, and every Saturday and Sunday they marveled at how wonderful it was to talk and be awake at the same time. One meandering weekend, Brandon suggested a radical way to carry the idyll into the week. "Let's have lunch," he proposed. "Twice a month. No matter what."

Jill thought this was a nice idea but never expected it would happen. After all, they had dated for four years before they were married, and although they worked down the block from each other for much of that time, they never once met for lunch. Since then they'd moved to offices a subway ride apart—his in midtown, hers near Spring and Lafayette, making a rendezvous even less likely. "I never even go to lunch," Jill said. "I eat a sandwich at my desk."

Enter Richard Ellenson, a pragmatic Manhattan realist. His advertising agency did business with Brandon's Web design agency, and because this was business, the two men did find time to dine out together. Over breakfast one morning, Brandon mentioned his twice-a-month-lunch plan and Richard laughed out loud. "It will never happen," he said, and pointed out that the breakfast they were sharing had been "rescheduled seven times in the past four weeks."

Richard wanted to make it clear that he has a romantic side. Although no longer a newlywed, he loves his wife and young son "passionately" and keeps their photo on the wall across from his desk, always in his line of sight. "I take little vacations every day," he said, describing how he pauses periodically to stare at that picture. But because his desk is in SoHo and his wife's is on the Upper East Side, that's the closest he has ever come to seeing her for lunch.

By the end of their breakfast, Brandon and Richard had made a bet: The skeptic would pay the newlywed one hundred dollars for every lunch beyond the twice-a-month goal in one year, and the newlywed would pay the skeptic one hundred dollars for every lunch below that number. Richard realized he had decreased his own odds by fortifying Brandon's determination with a bet. "I still have faith in the city of New York and faith in the power of stress," he said, "that even with all this monetary incentive, Brandon will not be able to make this work."

Bruce and I have been married for fourteen years. We

have had lunch during the workweek a total of seven times in all those years, and most of those were in a hospital cafeteria when someone in the family was in intensive care. Even under those stressful circumstances the time together was a treat. Yet it never occurred to us to lunch for no reason when all our relatives were healthy. This track record left me inclined to agree with Richard that work and marriage can't occupy the same space at the same time. But then I spoke to Brandon Lowitz.

He made it clear that this was not just a romantic whim, nor did it have much to do with lunch. The four hours a month that he planned to take from work and donate back to his marriage were his reminder to himself of what's important. "I don't believe that my life should be totally consumed by my work," he said. He understood that life only gets more complicated from here, and he saw this plan as carving inviolable space for himself and his wife, a buffer against future drains on their time. "It's like going to the gym," he said. "No one has enough time for it, but if you get the routine down, somehow it happens."

I didn't have the heart to mention that I hadn't been to the gym in months and that my exercise came from walking the dog and pacing with worry about work. That said, the Lowitzes didn't get off to a promising start. Brandon was traveling the week after he shook hands on his bet, but he penciled Jill in for lunch on the following Tuesday, at the Dean & DeLuca next to her office. After their lunch they planned to fax the receipt to Richard Ellenson.

Keep reading. My money is on them.

FIREWALLS

"How was your day?" my husband asks me every night when he finally makes his way home from the hospital. On my bad days—ones that involve deadlines, or spats with editors, or sources who won't cooperate—I grumble and grouse in reply.

"How was *yours?*" I remember to ask when I've finished complaining. On his bad days he'll say something like, "We lost a patient. He died on the list."

Bruce's patients are children with heart disease, many of whom are waiting for transplants, and some of whom don't receive one in time. "How old?" I ask, because I've come to understand that there is little else to say. Whatever the answer, I vow silently (and for the umpteenth time) never to lose perspective again.

Those of us who think we have hard jobs can learn a lot from those who really do. Lessons about separating work from life and about how much of ourselves we can give at the office so that we still have something left to give at home. How do some among us counsel rape victims, or investigate murder scenes, or dive for airplane wreckage all week, then have the energy to cheer for the high school soccer team on Sunday afternoon? How does a pediatric cardiologist, or a paramedic, or an AIDS doctor lose a young patient during the day, then calmly and sanely tuck his own sons in that night?

I've had a taste of this pain-by-proxy over the years. Much of my reporting has been about medical issues, which means I've learned to approach families in crisis and ask for permission to enter their lives. I've chronicled the agony of a young man with incurable tuberculosis, then stood in the operating room as one of his diseased lungs was surgically scraped from his chest. While researching a book about a hospital's ethics committee, I've sat with numb and weeping parents who had decided to remove the ventilator from their suffering baby daughter. I've interviewed murderers and the families of their victims; I've watched rescuers dig the living and the dead from a collapsed department store; I've cried with the school bus driver who accidentally plowed through a guardrail along a deep pit filled with water, causing dozens of children to drown.

I left each of these moments emotionally battered and bruised. I've also left exquisitely aware that I could walk away. I was an observer, not a participant—not the doctor, or the chaplain, or the rescue worker; not anyone expected to have answers. Tomorrow I could write about someone happy and content—the circus, perhaps, or chocolate. But what about those who can't move on to something else? How do you cope when your job requires going back for more the next day and the day after that? If those of us with more mundane jobs can't do it, can't keep the stress of work from oozing over and staining the rest of life, then how can they? More to the point, if they *can* do it, then why on earth can't we?

Whenever I've asked these heroes for their secrets, they talk simply but forcefully about perspective. "This ward is a trip to hell," says the Reverend Carolyn Yard, the chaplain at the Burn Center at New York Weill Cornell Medical Center who remembers spending her first day cradling a four-year-old whose dripping wounds were caused by lye his mother had thrown. "When you've seen hell, you don't mind a few earthly problems."

Even more than that, they talk about building walls and creating distance. While I was writing my book about a hospital, a young pediatrician explained that she chose neonatology over pediatric oncology because she became too attached to the older cancer patients (they reminded her of her own little brother). But she found she could separate emotionally from the tiny preemies (who looked, to her, more like patches of flesh than like people). "You need emotional armor," she said. "You draw a line and say, 'I'll give this much of myself, but no more.' "

Now, this is not the kind of talk we want to hear from our doctors or chaplains or, for that matter, our baby-sitters, schoolteachers, or politicians. We want them to care about the job—about us—completely and to take it all home. We want work to consume them. We feel entitled to this because we don't often leave ourselves room for walls either. Work lays claim to our time and emotion, possessing us as completely as any spouse or child.

But those who do the hardest jobs know that walls are the secret. Not just because they are the only way to carve out space for a life, but also because they are the only way to do the job. Anne Wilde supervises volunteers at HelpLine, the city's busiest suicide hotline, where callers often spend hours threatening to pull the trigger or swallow the pills— then they hang up abruptly, leaving the hotline counselor helpless to do anything but imagine the worst.

New volunteers will scour the newspapers for days afterward, Anne told me, terrified they will find a mention of their lost caller. The people who last longest at this work, however, are the ones who stop looking. On the bad days, Anne has learned to go home and cook herself an elaborate dinner. "I chop and mince. It smells wonderful, it tastes wonderful, and it means I have something left to give when I go to work the next day."

And that is the lesson for the rest of us, those for whom work is not a matter of life and death but has the ability to use us up nonetheless. If you immerse totally, you drown, and the only way to get the work done is to come up for air periodically, to step back now and then. To wonder about a lost caller, but shut the door and cook. To mourn the lost patient, but smile for your sons. To turn off the computer, even on deadline, and simply be there for your husband, so you can both go back out tomorrow and do it all again.

BABIES

PREGNANT AT WORK

A certain Op-Ed columnist at *The New York Times* was often the first to know who in the newsroom was pregnant. There was a couch up in her tenth-floor office—a cozy, quiet space that she rarely ever used because she worked from home—and women down on the third floor learned they could crash there in the early weeks, when their conditions were still secret.

As hiding goes, this was not as bad as it used to be. Generations of workers have hidden their pregnancies, because, in the repressed old days, being pregnant usually meant being unemployed. My mother tells of friends from her first job who, years before becoming pregnant, began wearing A-line dresses to buy them time from inquiring stares when they actually needed maternity wear. She and the other teachers covered for each other when they needed to dash off in the middle of class to throw up.

Our reasons for hiding are different now. We don't worry what our bosses will do, so much as we worry about what they will think. After spending careers trying to prove that we're professionals and that our personal lives won't intrude on our work, we find ourselves occupying bodies that scream otherwise. We fear that colleagues and clients will dismiss us as less valuable, and we also fear they might be right. We are determined to do our prepregnancy share, when all we really want to do is sleep. We act like we feel fine when we really couldn't feel much worse. We exhaust ourselves pretending we're the same as before, when everything about us is different.

I've known women who glow when they're pregnant. I was not one of them. I've also known women who are confident and at peace about their pending parenthood. I was terrified. If I hadn't already felt nauseated from the hormones, I probably would have been nauseated with nerves. I went into pregnancy with waffling ambivalence; my life was perfect, I protested, why change it? But after four years of marriage my husband and my parents, and his parents, and our grandparents (to name just a few) all seemed to think I wasn't getting any younger and promised life would be even more perfect once the next generation was underway.

On the chance they were right, I went ahead and got pregnant. Just in case they were wrong, I did the mature thing and I hid. Not on a couch on the tenth floor, but in a whole different city. We were still living in Houston at the time, which meant no one from what I considered the real world—namely the newsroom in New York—could see me. To this day my editors have no idea how often I answered their questions while lying on the floor trying not to retch.

In my seventh week they asked me to fly to Louisiana and profile the governor. I managed the turbulent plane ride and the bouncy trip in from the airport, but I didn't have the energy to go any further. So I curled up on the bed in my Baton Rouge hotel room and did the interview by phone. (The dateline on the story read BATON ROUGE, LA., which, at the time, was all that mattered.)

Then, in my seventh month, business brought me to New York. I looked a lot like the Pillsbury Doughboy by then, and although I had told everyone my news, I spent hours choosing an outfit that might make me seem less pregnant. I'm pretty sure it didn't work. I'm also sure there were unwanted pats on my belly and a handful of other less-than-professional moments, exactly as I had feared, but ten years later I honestly don't remember them. What I do remember in sharp detail is this: As I sat in a meeting discussing the details of an upcoming project my baby began to kick. It was a rhythmic beat, and it packed a wallop. The meeting went on around me as my boy went boom-boom-boom.

This was a different kind of secret. Not something I wanted to hide, so much as something I felt no need to share. Not something that made me nauseated or nervous, but something that made me smile. Everyone else in the room was fully focused on the business at hand. Me, I was someplace else, dancing the cha-cha with my son.

INTERNET BABY

In my cache of embarrassing memories is this:

I was an achingly enthusiastic new reporter, and I was working on an article for which I needed to interview a certain social worker. The story was important to me and I wanted to finish it *now*. I called the woman, with my calendar at the ready, and tried to schedule a time when we might talk. She was booked full on Thursday and Friday, so I suggested Saturday. I can still hear the surprise in her pause and the apology in her tone when she told me that Saturday was her day off.

Her answer annoyed me, and I'm sure I let it show. Saturday was my day off, too, but I was willing to work. Why wasn't she? (No, I didn't say this out loud, but I thought it, which is almost as bad.) I didn't mind working Saturdays because I didn't mind working *every* day. I hadn't taken a vacation in two years. Every once in a while, when I looked up from my desk late in the evening, I would wonder where everybody else had gone. It honestly never occurred to me that they were home reading bedtime stories to their kids.

I had a flashback to this clueless former self when I first met Aaron Cohen. The founder of a company called Concrete Media, he was your average Internet workaholic. His hours, he said proudly, "are somewhere between management consulting and investment banking." In other words, an hour or two short of "all the time." He could do this because he had no children and because his wife, Nina del Rio, was an Internet workaholic, too.

Employees at Cohen's three-year-old company (which built Web sites, nurtured them, then declared them independent and moved on) all worked the way their boss worked. The staff of one hundred thirty could work like this because at the time I first wrote about them, not a single one of them had children, either.

Old-fashioned companies—ones from the Stone Age of five or six years ago—were a reflection of the real world. Older workers. Younger workers. Some without children. Some with grown children. The preoccupations of life were evenly spread so that everyone in the room wasn't worrying about finding a date, or a baby-sitter, or a college loan at the same time. Dot-coms, particularly in their heyday, were anything but the real world. They were frat houses or college dorms, and the entire staff grew up (or not) together.

But Aaron called to tell me that everyone at Concrete Media was about to grow up. He and Nina were having a baby. Ry Sidney Cohen was due any minute now, and even before he was born, he proved it's not just market forces or consumer demand that cause a company to change.

"My intention is to be a highly focused father," Aaron said the week before his son was born. "I understand that it's important to balance my life. I'm determined to figure out how to do it."

For practice, he started leaving the office in the middle of the day to attend every one of his wife's doctor appointments. He canceled all travel in the two months before and the two months after his wife's due date and insisted that a company off-site meeting, scheduled near B-Day, be rescheduled because he might not make it home in time should the baby decide to arrive. Instead of staying out late at high-profile dinners or having low-key drinks with employees, he started coming home to his very tired wife. There he could be found reading *"Fast Company, The Red Herring,* and T. Berry Brazelton at the same time" and worrying whether being a CEO will be of any use at all when it comes time to help his son with the newest version of new math.

Aaron's altered focus was felt at the office. Concrete Media had added ten new employees in the five months before the baby was due, all of whom were age thirty-eight or older. The "influx of grown-ups," Aaron explained, brought the median employee age to the late twenties, up from the mid-twenties. A number of the new employees were hired to create a benefits department, which the company did not yet have. It had no maternity/paternity policy either, though one was in the works, modeled on Aaron's plan to take off the week immediately after the baby's birth and a total of six weeks within the first six months of the boy's life.

There was also talk of a day care center in the new headquarters being readied for the company downtown. "Working parents need this," Aaron said with the fervor of the newly converted. "There would be such a demand if you could figure out how to do it right."

At thirty-three he had come to understand that maturity is a good thing. "We see this company as being around for a long, long time," he said. "We need to hit a stride that is sustainable over the long haul. If I can't learn how to be a parent and an executive, then I can't imagine how I can ask my employees to do that."

The transformation, while welcome, made some of his employees a little nervous. They weren't quite sure what to make of this man who expected to have a life. But those who worried that their boss is slowing down so much they will not recognize him could take solace in this: "We dropped out of Lamaze," Aaron said. "It was just too slow. I don't have that kind of patience. We'll read the books instead."

MATERNITY LEAVE

The acting governor of Massachusetts, Jane M. Swift, went on "working maternity leave" after she gave birth to her twins. The babies were delivered by cesarean section after her doctor affirmed that she would be awake and conscious so she didn't have to sign her authority over to anyone. The twins came a month early, and during the week of bedrest before they were born the thirty-four-year-old governor road-tested this working maternity leave concept by conducting meetings via teleconference.

As too many of us know, however, "working maternity leave" is just an oxymoronic label for what we already do. *True* maternity leave—months of bonding time uncluttered by calls from the office—is more the exception than the rule, because those of us paid well enough to afford the time are often too "indispensable" to take it, and those who could slip more easily out of work usually can't afford to. I spent my first maternity leave moving from the bureau in Houston to the newsroom in New York. I'm still not sure how someone moves a family halfway across the country while not on maternity leave. My second was spent frantically finishing a book, which (like my second child) was long overdue. My sister-in-law interrupted her second maternity leave to give three separate speeches about health care policy, which is her specialty. She brought the baby along, as well as the baby's grandmother, and then nursed in the lobby between conference sessions.

A handful of women wear this as a badge of female machismo (as in "I finalized a deal during fifteen hours of labor and was back in the office two days after the baby was born"). A few more are stunned to discover that their work defines them and they are eager to get back *now*. The rest of us do it simply because the work needs to be done. Amanda-Beth Uhry is the founder of a thriving public relations firm, and when she adopted her daughter, Arabella, from China years ago, she expected to take three months off. Instead, the minute she left the country to pick up her daughter "all hell broke loose" at work, she said, and she ran up a seven-hundred-dollar telephone bill from her Guangdong province hotel room, trying to run the office from twelve thousand miles away.

"I will always remember my maternity leave as not having maternity leave," said Amanda-Beth, who returned to work the day after she arrived back home. "It's supposed to be a time when you can bond with your child. I needed that time. I didn't even know that the cartoon part of the Pampers goes in front when you put on the diaper, and here I am handing her over to a baby-sitter from day one. I felt gypped."

Whereas Amanda-Beth learned that her work could not do without her, Patty Jackson realized that she cannot do without work—or, more specifically, without the paycheck

that her work brings. Patty, a DJ at WDAS-FM in Philadelphia, gave birth to Robert Joseph on the same day that Acting Governor Swift birthed her twins, also a month ahead of
schedule. Robert came home from the hospital on a Tuesday, and by the following Monday his mother was back on
the air—from a remote studio newly hooked up in her
home. "I'm a single mom, which means I'm the only bread-
winner," she explained the day before she returned to work.
At the time she vowed to be up-front with her listeners
about where she was and what she was doing. "I'm going to
tell people we're home," said Patty, who expected she'd disappear into her kitchen during long music sets and use her
breast pump, "and that the noise they hear in the background is the baby wanting to be fed."

Like Amanda-Beth Uhry, Governor Swift went back to
work because her job demanded it. Like Patty Jackson, she
also went back to work because she wanted to keep her job.
If she expected to become more than just the acting governor, she needed to improve her dismal popularity numbers,
which, at their lowest, showed that only 17 percent of voters
gave her a favorable rating. She had been in hot water in the
past for allowing her life to very publicly intrude upon her
work. As lieutenant governor she was fined by a state ethics
commission for having her aides baby-sit for her daughter,
and shortly after that, she was criticized for using a state hel-
icopter to fly home (her commute to the state house is 133
miles, or nearly three hours, one way by car) when that same
little girl fell ill.

Just before she gave birth this second time, one cranky
member of her Governor's Council, which provides advice

and consent on judicial appointments, challenged the constitutionality of any decisions made by teleconference during this "working maternity leave." More modern heads quickly prevailed. Maybe that's because we have finally arrived at a time when work can adapt itself to life. Or maybe it's just because all those men feared they might have to watch their governor breast-feed at a conference table.

PATERNITY LEAVE

I first realized I was morphing into a work-life advocate, not just a work-life reporter, when I became utterly irritated at Tony Blair. During one slow news cycle the baby-faced British prime minister was deciding (and deciding, and deciding) whether or not to take paternity leave when his fourth child arrived. Until then I had never thought much about paternity leave. Bruce took off a week from work when each of our sons was born, and then he slipped back easily into the working world. I'd been more than a bit jealous, I admit, that he got to spend the day with grown-ups, but I didn't see this as a philosophical gauntlet. Tony Blair's dithering, on the other hand, annoyed me.

"I've got a country to run," he sputtered to the BBC. "I honestly don't know what to do." That led to the predictable jokes about nappies and a less predictable debate over the importance of paternity leave—a spanking-new concept in Britain, which boasts a new law allowing parents up to thirteen weeks of unpaid time off from work during the first five years of a child's life.

The loudest voices urged Blair to go for it. SHOW NEW DADS THE WAY, TONY! screamed a front-page headline in *The Mirror*, which argued that Blair had a duty to spend at least one week at home. His wife seemed to agree. Cherie Blair— a high-powered lawyer with ambitions to be a High Court judge—quite publicly praised Finnish Prime Minister Paavo Lipponen for taking off six whole days after his wife gave birth to their second child. "I, for one, am promoting a widespread adoption of this fine example," said Mrs. Blair, who, for the record, planned to take at least thirteen weeks.

Here on this side of the Atlantic, certain circles were watching closely. We, too, have a law (the 1993 Family and Medical Leave Act) intended to encourage paternity leave, but so far it has not sent men home to their newborns in droves. One poll found that although a decisive majority of us believe that fathers should take more than two weeks of paternity leave, 71 percent of us couldn't think of any male friend or relative who had actually done this.

That's mostly because here (as in Britain) the law fails to put any money where its mouth is, providing only for unpaid leave. But it is also because changing the law is not the same as changing the culture.

"Women who take time off are seen as responding to a higher calling," said author Suzanne Braun Levine. "Men who take time off are seen as being henpecked and letting the operation down."

Ms. Levine spoke to scores of men for her book, *Father Courage: What Happens When Men Put Family First,* and concluded that those who do stay home with their newborns disguise it as something else—unused vacation, comp time, sick leave. What men need, she decided, was a good role model, and she thought the British prime minister would do just fine.

But what would he be an example of? This was the part that got my goat. To hear some of the talk on this side of the pond, you'd think he was to be lauded simply for being so darn supportive. "He should take some time off and help his wife with the wee one," suggested one editorial. Hmm. How nice of him to *help*. And how *helpful* his wife had been, earning an estimated three times his salary these past few years.

It would be more constructive, I thought, to turn the focus to the "wee one." In her book *Flux: Women on Sex, Work, Love, Kids & Life in a Half-Changed World*, Peggy Orenstein cites studies showing that the more time men spend alone with a baby during the early months—and we're talking full-time here, not "helping" Mom when she takes an hour off to run to the supermarket—the more involved they are as parents for all the years afterward. "Paternity leave has lifelong benefits to a child," she says. "Why aren't women storming the ramparts over this?"

Why indeed? And why didn't it occur to my husband—an otherwise enlightened and liberated man—to take more than a few days away from work to meet each of his sons? Women who manage to take maternity leave do so for only one reason—because they want the time with their new babies. If it were just a time for physical recovery, we'd all dash back to work after six weeks, tops. Yet nothing I read, no talk show chat that I heard, suggested that time with his baby is a gift Blair should give to *himself*.

"I did it because I couldn't imagine not doing it," said Ed Tagliaferri, a longtime reporting friend of mine, of the three weeks he cobbled from vacation time and comp time seven years ago when his son was born. "I wanted to experience it all and throw myself into it from the start."

Tony Blair never took that paternity leave. But he should have. Not just because it would have set a good example. And not only because studies show it would be good for his child. But simply because he *wanted* to. What better role for the rest of us to model?

LOVE

AND WORK

AND MARRIAGE

AND BABIES

WORKING MOM

My mother worked, and I turned out okay. In fact, my mother worked a lot. She was a teacher until I was born, then she added a Ph.D. in psychology, followed by a law degree and a legal career that would have made her father proud. Eventually she entered the international insurance business. No, I don't understand what an international insurance expert does any more than I understand what an international lawyer does, but it certainly gets her lots of frequent-flier miles.

My mother worked, and I turned out okay. I recited this like a mantra through nine months of pregnancy. Not only did she work, but she loved working, and yet . . . we had dinner each night as a family (takeout, usually, but let's not quibble). I never came home to an empty house after school. There was always someone to help with my homework (or bring it to school when I forgot it) or pick me up and tuck me in when I was sick.

My mother worked, and I turned out okay. Within days after Evan was born, I knew he would be okay, too. One afternoon I loaded him into his stroller intending to sit in the broiling sun in the courtyard of our Houston apartment building and edit a manuscript while he slept. The elevator was broken. I had to bounce the stroller down the stairs. He woke up on the very last step, and his screams were accompanied by the unmistakable sound of a diaper being dirtied. I carried the stroller back up the stairs, changed the diaper, nursed him back to sleep, then collapsed in a miserable, sweaty heap on the couch.

Yes, Evan's mother would work, and Evan would be okay. But whether his *mother* would be okay was far from certain.

When our native Texan was three months old we moved back to New York and took up the life of suburban commuters. It was a life led to the rhythm of a portable breast pump and the whistle of the early-evening train. Missing the 6:19 from Grand Central meant missing bedtime and bathtime at home. Some nights that broke my heart. Other nights I was secretly relieved (but racked with guilt at my relief) that there'd be that much less for me to do when I finally made it home.

"How did you do it?" I asked my mother in a tone that was more accusation than compliment. "How did you study for the bar exam and keep us fed? How did you write your thesis and proofread our homework? How come your generation did it and mine is losing its collective mind?"

In the world according to Mom, the answer is threefold. First, she says, my life really is more complicated. She was a mother first. Then she had a career. She didn't graduate from law school until I was a senior in high school. When her youngest child left for college, Mom was forty-two years old and there was no one waiting at home for a bath and a story. When I am forty-two my youngest will still be in elementary school. Mom did things serially while my generation does them simultaneously.

That said, Mom gently suggests that me and mine all think too much. Working mothers, she reminds us, have always felt torn. It's just that there are more of us now, in jobs that are more fulfilling partly because they are more demanding, and we are not a group who sees a need to shoulder our frustrations quietly. There is a hint of reprimand in her voice when she says this. Her own mother worked, and she turned out okay—but there were times when her parents just couldn't be there. "That's why they call it work," she says, quoting my grandmother.

But the most important difference between my life and hers, the reason I felt like a failure and she felt like an adventurer, is a difference I came to see only after I had children of my own. When I look back on my childhood, I remember the security of knowing someone was always there. What my naïve eyes didn't notice was who that someone was. When my mother wasn't home, my *father* was, straightening patients' teeth in his suite of offices attached to the house, greeting me when I came off the school bus every afternoon, bringing my homework when I forgot it (truth be told, he sent his receptionist to do that, but I was relieved to be rescued), and tucking me in when I was sick.

Yes, my mother worked, and I turned out okay.

Thank you, Mom and Dad.

BABY-SITTERS

Evan's first baby-sitter was named Chanpheng. Hers is a Laotian name, and when it's pronounced properly, which I don't seem able to do, it sounds like "champagne." That's fitting because hers was a sweet, effervescent presence in my life.

She took care of my baby, yes, but she also took care of me. I had neither bathed nor diapered an infant before I had one of my own, and I'd held newborns only when they were thrust upon me by besotted postpartum friends. Chanpheng, though younger than I was, had done it all. Every morning she came with her son and two daughters. Together they cooed in a circle around Evan, tickling his belly and kissing his toes for hours. While they did this I took a shower or wrote a few paragraphs, whichever seemed more urgent on that particular day.

Chanpheng was only in our lives for three months before we moved away. We left dozens of dear friends in Houston, a city we'd come to think of as our home. But the only tears I shed during all the good-byes were when I brought Evan to see Chanpheng and her children one last time.

The most important woman in any working mother's life is her baby-sitter. "I need a wife," I sometimes joke when the list of must-dos grows too long. What I'd prefer is a clone, but practical, ethical, and legal obstacles being what they are, I've turned instead to Chanpheng and Debbie, Chrissy and Bernice, Luan and Marielle. When my sons grow into happy, fulfilled, loving adults it will be because of these women. And if I am still sane and standing when they reach adulthood, my baby-sitters will get the credit for that, too.

There is no template for what we are to each other, my baby-sitter and me. Employer-employee? It's more intimate than that. Confidantes and friends? Not quite *that* intimate. At its core it is a business relationship, because I pay her and she answers to me. (Like most managers, she has all the responsibility when she's with my children but none of the final authority.) That said, this particular strain of business relationship starts off with a sheaf of questions that are probably prohibited in business—Do you have children? Do you want to have them? How religious are you? How were you disciplined as a child?—but these are your children you are handing over to this stranger, so you ask away. In fact, the only question that you do not ask is the only one you really want answered: "Will you love my children the way I do, and will they learn to love you almost as much as they love me?"

The one thing I've never admitted to any baby-sitter, because I've barely admitted it to myself, is that I don't want her to be everything to my children that I am. I want her to be more than I am and everything I am not. I want her to be consistently cheerful and endlessly patient, sitting on the floor all afternoon playing the age-appropriate equivalent of patty-cake. I want her to enforce the "the no TV until after homework, dinner, and shower" rule even though I have been known to give in because it's easier. I want her to insist on nutritious snacks after school, when I might be tempted to permit sugar and salt. I want her to ride the scariest roller coasters at Great Adventure, so that I don't have to, and to play soccer on the front lawn without ever saying, "Maybe later, sweetie, I have to work." It would take a therapist all of five minutes to figure out that I feel guilty offering my children a Mommy replacement, and to assuage my guilt I need to believe they are in better hands with her than with me.

No human being could be all that I might want, but over the years our sitters have blessed Evan and Alex, in their own ways. Bernice, nurturing and sweet, lay in the window seat for hours with a baby blissfully asleep on her chest. Chrissy, bubbly and athletic, was their cheerleader when they learned to ride their bikes. Marielle, quiet and patient, sang them lullabies in French. And Debbie had the look. One glance from that woman and children for miles around would happily and obediently do whatever they were asked. I'm still trying to have the same effect.

As they become enmeshed in my children's lives, I become enmeshed in theirs. Bruce says, only half-jokingly, that I spend more time worrying about the baby-sitter's happiness than I spend worrying about his. That's because I'm fairly certain that if he were feeling frustrated or depressed he would mention it, and I'm equally certain that my baby-sitter would not. She might take it out on my children instead. So I take her emotional temperature regularly and often, making it even harder to tell where the boundaries of her life blend into ours.

Debbie married and had a baby during the years she cared for us, and I felt more than a boss's joy and pride as I watched her life take shape. My boys went through sibling rivalry when she was pregnant, but they came to love baby Harriett like a sister. They made it clear that Debbie's house, with a baby to play with, was much more fun than their own, and they periodically asked to move in.

Harriett was two months old when Debbie broke the news that she'd decided to shorten her workweek to four days, from five. I was racing to finish a book at the time, and I needed her *eight* days a week, not four. A boss would have said no. A boss would have found a new worker who could do the entire job. Instead, with Debbie's help, I cobbled alternate arrangements for the boys on Friday afternoons—relying on friends, grandparents, and high schoolers, all of whom had complicated schedules of their own. But on weeks when all else failed, and particularly on those Fridays when I was out of town, Debbie stepped in and took the boys for an extra afternoon.

We juggled our calendars like this for several months, until her husband changed jobs and she and her family moved away. She was followed by Chrissy, a student working her way to a psychology degree, who didn't want to even think about babies until she finished school and opened her own child care center. What she *did* want, however, was to fly home for Christmas and stay there through New Year's—if that would be convenient.

Well, I had a deadline smack in the middle of those ten days, and my husband was on call. But she was wonderful with the boys, and we were lucky to have her, so she booked her nonrefundable ticket and I blocked out an unscheduled vacation. I figured I would work late at night and early in the morning if I really had to. And, for extra insurance, I wrote about the whole dilemma in a column that ended "if my first column of the new year is a little late, I'm sure my own boss will understand . . ."

THE GRAPES OF
MARITAL WRATH

Robin Klein, a senior vice president at Chase Manhattan Bank, is loathe to let her husband go grocery shopping. "I've tried, but even when I make a detailed list, he'll bring home the wrong brand or the cottage cheese that's salt-free and you can't eat," she told a banquet room full of similarly frustrated women over dinner one night. She was still recovering from the day that her otherwise sharp-as-a-tack spouse (an accomplished executive with impeccable business sense) came home with two pounds of grapes that were turning brown. "I went ballistic," she remembered. "I was ranting like a lunatic over three dollars' worth of grapes."

It is easy to look at this scene through a men-don't-get-it-and-women-are-left-doing-everything lens. That's certainly the way all we chuckling women at that dinner saw it. But Naomi R. Cahn, who tries to take the more academic view, suggests we look into a mirror instead.

Professor Cahn studies workplace obstacles to equality between the sexes. She was immersed in her research over at George Washington University Law School a while back when she was struck by the fact that she so often interrupted her own work to, say, make play dates for her preschool daughters. Her husband, on the other hand, would simply go to work and do his *work*.

This realization led her to change the direction of her research and study the homefront, too. That, in turn, led to scholarly journal articles in which she argued that there can't be true equality in the workplace until there is also equality at home. And among the obstacles to equality at home— deep breath, here comes the tricky part—are women themselves. "Workplace change," she wrote, "will be hampered until women relinquish some of the power that they have at home."

Now, before you write an outraged letter to the professor (or to me, I'm just the messenger), listen for a moment to what she did not say. She didn't suggest that this is only the women's fault, or that society in general is blameless, or that men are not a large chunk of the problem. (To the contrary, she believes that some men—you know who you are— deliberately bungle chores so no one asks them a second time.) But she did write that one ingredient in the social stew is the difficulty that so many women have giving up certain kinds of control.

Sociologists even have a name for this. "It's called 'gatekeeping,'" said Joan Williams, author of *Unbending Gender: Why Family and Work Conflict and What to Do About It,* when I approached her with Professor Cahn's theory. "It describes a situation in which a woman really feels she should be the central person in her children's lives." However, given the complexities of real life, she continued, a woman also "holds her husband to the standard of equal parenting." What results, she suggested, are scuffles over things like bruised grapes.

This talk of gatekeeping hits a little close to my own (well-guarded) front gate. Remember the visit INS workers made to the father of Elián González? Among the questions they asked was what size shoe the boy wore. Because Mr. González knew the answer, he was deemed a fit parent. I waved a newspaper account of that meeting like a banner at our house—imagine, a father who knows a child's shoe size!

But were I to look in Naomi Cahn's mirror I would have to face the fact that my husband knows how to buy shoes. In fact, he leaves the house every day wearing shoes he chose all by himself. Given his years of complex and technical training as a pediatrician, he even knows not to get the boys sandals in February. So he might well know his sons' shoe sizes—if only I'd let him buy them shoes once in a while. Instead, I've put a fence around shoe shopping (and birthday party planning and yearly checkups and arranging play dates . . .). Then I stand inside the gate and vent about how I have a full-time job, too, and why does the burden of the "second shift" fall on me.

It was Arlie Hochschild who first coined that phrase in her book by the same name. She quantified how women in the workplace come home at night to a second full-time job. My children's shoes, she told me, stand for all the things I worry I am not doing for my boys. "Certain acts of motherhood"—usually ones we can no longer do—"become hypersymbolized," she said, and "we have to learn to let that symbolism fall away."

Robin Klein is trying. She told her story about the grapes at a meeting of a group called Second Shift—one hundred professional women from my neighborhood who gather for dinner and conversation several times a year. After admitting her problem, she pledged to work toward a solution. Sounding like a new member at a twelve-step meeting, she took the microphone and promised to inch open the gate. "I'm reminding myself, 'It doesn't matter if the grapes are bruised,'" she said, to knowing laughter and applause. True, this isn't the solution to unequal pay or glass ceilings or lack of corporate child care. But it's a start.

BROCCOLI AND SAUCE

Call it "The Broccoli Problem." Every few months, dozens of business executives travel to the Wharton School at the University of Pennsylvania for an intensive week spent sharpening their negotiation skills. That they are sent by their companies is a sign of their authority. These folks are important. It is their job to tell other people what to do.

Which is why it is so striking to G. Richard Shell, the professor who runs the seminar, to hear what these commanding folks have to say when they introduce themselves at the opening dinner. Asked to explain why they've come, they often talk of frustrations that have nothing to do with work: a daughter who won't clean her room, a son who doesn't respect curfew, a toddler who refuses to eat her vegetables. All this crackerjack talent at the office. Why doesn't it work for them at home?

From the time I first started to work, I noticed that my working self has a different personality than my nights-and-weekends self. It's not a change as dramatic as Jekyll and Hyde. More like Mr. Rogers trading his jacket for his sneakers and cardigan, or maybe Superman changing out of his flashy suit, because I seem to lose some of my "power" in the process. After spending all day smoothly interviewing grown-ups, for instance, I can then spend all evening being stonewalled by my smallest source. "Nothing," he answers, with all the force of a politician's "no comment," when I ask him what he did in second grade that day.

I've come to see this as a necessary transformation. The alternative, to my mind, is Captain von Trapp in *The Sound of Music,* whistling for his children as he would whistle for his sailors. So when Professor Shell poses his question—"Why doesn't it work for them at home?"—I am ready with an answer. Home and job are different. The skill sets that work in one are useless in the other.

Wrong, said the professor. Skills from the office work just fine at home—if only we would remember to use them.

As the author of *Bargaining for Advantage: Negotiation Strategies for Reasonable People,* the specific skills he means are ones of negotiation. Imagine, he said, that you are a manager who needs an employee to work weekends. Would you yell at that employee? Would you set the kitchen timer and let it tick until he agrees? Would you send him to his cubicle or tell him he can't have dessert? Now imagine you are trying to get a serving of broccoli into a child who's locked his jaw. Wouldn't you do all of those things?

Of course you would, Professor Shell said, and you would do so because you are human. It is tiring to keep going at home as you have in the office—which is why the cobbler's children of folklore have no shoes. "I can't drill my son at night the way I drill my students during the day," a reading teacher once told me, worrying over the irony that her son was behind the curve in his own reading skills. "I want to be his mother."

Not only are we too tired to bring our professional selves home, Professor Shell said, we are also too emotional. A good manager would be thinking of compromise, trying to give the employee some modicum of control, such as a choice of which weekend to work. That manager would also have a Zen understanding of the fact that this is just a scheduling conflict—not a reflection of his value as a human being. But for a parent, each stalk of broccoli becomes all that stands between the child and scurvy, and each uneaten bite is proof positive that this child will grow up to be an undisciplined brat.

I was about to argue with Professor Shell, to point out that I don't know a lot of Zen-like managers (most simply offer extra pay for a weekend of work, which isn't exactly the right message for a toddler) and that maybe an excess of emotion at home is what makes it a home. Do we really want razor-sharp vision or analytical acuity when gazing at our families, or do we want things to be blurred by a little love?

In other words, I was about to redefine imperfection and weakness as a deliberate life's choice. But then the professor mentioned that he had successfully negotiated the broccoli problem with his own younger son, and I was distracted by the details.

The secret, it seems, is a package of McDonald's Sweet 'N Sour Sauce.

Try pouring *that* over an unpalatable weekend shift.

TAKE OUR DAUGHTERS
TO WORK, 2000

Every year, nineteen million girls play hooky from school for a lesson their parents consider even more important. It's called Take Our Daughters to Work Day, and it was created to give adolescent girls a peek at a limitless future.

I used to be a girl. And, as books that were not even written back then would have predicted, I lost much confidence in myself—and all interest in math—at the stroke of age twelve. (Most of the confidence has come back; not so for the math.) As a former girl, and as a feminist and defender of girls, I am thrilled by Take Our Daughters to Work Day. But as the mother of two young sons, I am torn.

I do not for a moment question that this is good for girls. "It's a national intervention," said Marie Wilson, president of the Ms. Foundation for Women, which created the day. "It sends a positive message to girls and focuses on their potential." That message is only heard, she added, "if the boys are not there. Otherwise the boys take over and everyone reverts to the behaviors we are trying to address in the first place."

Okay, but let's stop for a moment and talk about those boys. If we as a country have learned anything since Columbine, it is that they are in trouble, too. They are shooting and being shot, using drugs and being medicated for behavioral disorders far more than their sisters. As parents we are frightened for them.

Even Mary Bray Pipher, author of *Reviving Ophelia: Saving the Selves of Adolescent Girls,* has warned that it is time to pay more attention to the boys. "An event like this comes out of a certain place and time," she said, treading carefully, trying not to directly attack Take Our Daughters to Work Day. "But the further you get from that place and time, the less likely it is to be fitting and appropriate. No one would make the argument now that boys have an easy time in middle school and high school."

What I wrestle with, I admit, is less the welfare of all boys than the specific needs of two particular boys: Alex, who once insisted that girls can't be doctors (even though two of his pediatricians are women) but who is fascinated by the fact that one of my editors is a "he" and one is a "she"; and Evan, who loves to compare the techniques I use in my articles with the ones he uses when writing his reports on the Arctic and the Amazon.

Every night they ask me, "How was your day?" Would it be a boon or a blow to feminism if, once a year, I show them?

Marie Wilson, the mother of three sons and two daughters, answered that it would be a little of both. Although she is all for raising feminist sons, she warned that the trend toward companies opting for Take Our *Children* to Work Days is diluting the point. The Ms. Foundation, she explained, has created a separate program—Working It Out: Especially for Boys—to be taught to those who are left in the classroom while the girls head off to the workplace. But if my children's school is at all typical, the program is not widely used, and the day is a wasted one for the boys.

"I can't teach anything new that day," said my son's third-grade teacher when I asked her advice. Added his principal, in her strictest principal voice: "Why on earth do they schedule this during the school year? You know, it's *not* a legal absence."

No, but done right it can be an educational one. It certainly is at *The New York Times,* where each year hundreds of daughters energize the building with their presence and produce their own remarkable newspaper. It's called *Girls Times,* and three years ago its lead editorial was an impassioned plea to end a practice it called "needlessly discriminatory."

"Times have changed," the girls wrote. "Daughters already know they can become lawyers, engineers, or golf professionals. . . . Sons as well as daughters can benefit from seeing what their fathers and mothers do at work." In the title of their editorial they advised "Take Your Sons to Work, Too."

With apologies to the principal, I took that advice. Evan spent the day with me, helping me conduct interviews for an upcoming magazine piece, then joining me back home in my office (so as not to intrude on the structured girls' program in the newsroom), where we each wrote an article about what we'd learned. And next year—fair is fair—I promised that it would be Alex's turn.

TAKE OUR DAUGHTERS
TO WORK, 2001

A year passed and Take Our Daughters to Work Day rolled around again. The girls were back, swarming the workplace, all training to be impassioned, emboldened adults. This second time around I found myself wrestling with a deeper conflict. Once we take our children to work, or start talking to them about work, what exactly do we say?

We could teach them that work is fulfilling and enriching. That there is satisfaction in a job well done and that they can accomplish anything, if they are willing to work for it. Inevitably, however, they will be faced with a task that is not fulfilling but tedious and hard. Do we risk raising a generation that can't cope with honest labor because they were brought up only to follow their bliss? Kids know we are lying, because if work is so rewarding, then why are grown-ups so grumpy every night? And if we really can be whatever we choose, then why isn't everyone a major league ballplayer?

The other choice is to come clean and teach them that work is hard. That it can be difficult and dull, and it takes parents away from home when they would rather be reading bedtime stories, but that it still has to be done. Work puts food on the table, and pays for orthodonture, and we do it because Great-Grandpa didn't take Great-Grandma's advice and buy real estate cheap during the Depression. But this means we are raising them to dread what they will probably do for nearly all of their lives. And what's wrong with growing up wanting to play major league ball anyway?

I remember the moments I first realized how I love the clatter of the newsroom—the daily race to the finish line, the heady fear of stumbling, the exhilaration of staying on my feet. I also remember my naïve annoyance when I realized I would have to write what I was assigned. I saw that same look of awe on Evan's face when he first fell into reading years ago—devouring books, immersing himself in the pages. (Thank you J. K. Rowling.) And I saw a reminder of my own bewilderment and defiance when he realized he would have to read whatever books the teacher chose, even if they were stupid and boring.

It was just one of what will be a lifetime of conflicting messages. Mommy loves her writing, I told him at age six, but if you don't leave my office now and let me work I'll lose my job. Play the saxophone because you love it, I tell him now, at age eleven, but if you don't love it today you still have to march upstairs and practice anyway. A summer job as a camp counselor sounds like fun, I might tell him at age sixteen, but wouldn't an internship with a nuclear physicist look better on a college application?

It was F. Scott Fitzgerald who wrote that "the test of a first-rate intelligence is the ability to hold two opposed ideas in the mind at the same time and still retain the ability to function." While I'm not quite certain that I'm fully functional, I do look at work and see two contradictory truths at once. Even at its very best, it is both a way to define ourselves and a necessary evil. On Take Our Daughters to Work Day we are given a chance to see our work through our children's eyes. Maybe the real purpose of the day is not to show the girls that work can be enriching and fun, but to remind ourselves, as well.

TAKE YOUR PARENT
TO WORK DAY, 2001

In the conference room at Vault.com's downtown office one chilly afternoon there were graying heads and relaxed-fit jeans in numbers that had never been seen there before. There were cookies and milk, too, and a PowerPoint video demonstration that began with the basics and got simpler. "What is the Internet?" the first slide asked. Answer: "A bunch of computers that are connected together."

So began Take Your Parent to Work Day at Vault.com, the first of what may become a yearly event to explain to parents what the heck their children do for a living. It was a day born of a pattern that starts back in kindergarten, when they first evade your questions about what they did at school. By the time they graduate, odds are you wouldn't understand the answer, particularly if they've entered one of those parallel work universes that didn't yet exist back when you got your first job.

Vault.com was just such a place, a three-year-old career guidance Web site, with about one hundred employees. It was the kind of break-down-the-walls company where the head of human resources is called the chief people officer and where the average age of the staff was twenty-four before fifty-eight-year-old Eric Ober, balding and avuncular, was brought in as CEO.

"My name is Eric," he said, opening this meeting, "and I'm the adult supervision here. It should reassure you that there is an adult working with your children. And don't worry," he added. "My mother doesn't have a clue what I do, either."

He introduced his mother, Sara Silverman, who agreed that she was clueless on this subject, then explained that this is not because of ignorance, but out of choice. "If I were seventeen instead of eighty-seven I would try to learn," she said. "I don't need a computer. I'd rather go to a book to look something up. I'd rather use an encyclopedia or something that I can hold in my hand."

She came on this day, she said, so she could describe what her son does when friends and relatives ask. "Dot-com this, dot-com that," she said. "I hear all these names thrown around and so many of them seem to be having money problems now. I want to know, how do they put the material into the computer and how do they take it out? Who calls them to find out what? How do people know about this company in order to call it in the first place?

"When Eric was vice president of CBS News, I understood where he worked," she continued. "When he was at the Food Network, I understood that, too. But I'm very confused by this."

Vault.com had three founders, brothers Samar Hamadeh and H. S. Hamadeh, and their college roommate, Mark Oldman. They all brought their mothers, too. Although the

Hamadehs said their mom was savvy enough with a computer to send an occasional E-mail, Mark described his mother as "a technophobe. I tell her about the business, but I water it down so she can understand. If she would give it a chance, she would get it." Mothers, he said, "are made for E-mail. It's a wonderful way of staying in touch all the time. Isn't that what mothers want to do?"

Dr. Marilyn Oldman confirmed that she doesn't do E-mail and had never been to her son's Web site. ("My ex-husband was addicted to the computer," she said. "When I divorced him, I thought, I don't need this in my life.") She did relish being invited to visit her son's company, however, and she even came prepared with an embarrassing story (because that's also "what mothers do"). "When he was six," she began, "he refused to go to summer camp; he insisted he had work to do. He started looking up companies in the phone book and putting on a deep voice. They sent samples of things to the house. He even had a salt representative come to his school and explain how the product was made."

After the slide show and the cookies, the parents were given a tour of the company's open, unpretentious offices. Mark's mother, who had visited before, said she was impressed by the "energetic, happy" feel of the place. In her psychology practice, she said, "I treat a lot of upset and stressed-out employees for large corporations. Mark provides a democratic and very enthusiastic environment." Was that because Mark asked her advice on employee morale? Well, no. "He was brought up by me," his mother answered, "with my values and standards and outlook on life."

Eric's mother, who was there for the first time, wondered why there were no walls in the loftlike space, and, as a result, no real offices. In this world, seniority is signaled by a filing cabinet separating top-ranking management from every-one else. When he worked at CBS, she said, her son "had a real office, with a big beautiful desk and soft chairs." Never fear, someone told her, "this means he's moving up in the world."

BRINGING

LIFE TO WORK

MORE LUNCH

Several months went by with no word from Jill and Brandon Lowitz, the two starry-eyed newlyweds who vowed to step out of the rat race twice a month and meet each other for lunch. I planned to check in with them as their yearlong bet with Richard Ellenson neared its end, but one morning, halfway through that year, Brandon called me out of the blue. His voice was giddy with mischief.

At first, he said, things had gone well for the lovers. They dined at intimate little bistros in SoHo, always extending the lunch hour by thirty minutes or more, and never, ever talking about work. When they sent Richard their receipts they scribbled arrogant, triumphant notes on top. Slowly, though, real life began to get in the way. Brandon's job in business development for a dot-com and his wife's job in marketing for a fashion designer meant meetings and business trips intruded upon lunch.

"It's a lot harder than we'd thought," Brandon admitted. "We each have crazy schedules, and they are not always crazy at the same time."

By the time six months had passed, when they should have had twelve lunches (literally) under their belt, they had managed to squeeze in only six. Then Brandon's company hit rough road and laid off 40 percent of its workforce. Although he did not lose his job, he did lose his enthusiasm for it. He had been at the start-up for four years, an eternity in the Internet business, and it was draining to watch his life's work wither. "It's like a live plant and then suddenly nobody's going to water it anymore," he said.

Walking home along Avenue A one particularly frustrating day, he decided he did not want to be "a dog chasing its tail" anymore. At the corner of Eighth Street he called his wife from his cell phone and suggested they both quit their jobs and move to Bali. By the time he reached the corner of Seventh Street she had agreed.

A few days after this call, Brandon took another walk, this time with the founder of his company, and announced he was quitting. "I'm out of gas," he said. "I don't have any more fuel in my tank." The next day, Jill dropped her own bomb at work. Afterward, she said, "I skipped all the way home. Everyone tells me we're doing what they have always dreamed of."

The days after that were filled with preparations for their escape. They bought two open-ended tickets to Bali via Bangkok, booked a villa for their first week, found South East Asian cooking classes and woodcarving classes on-line, and went to the bank for Indonesian rupee and Thai baht. In the midst of all these errands, they also made time to pause for lunch—with Richard Ellenson and me.

Over gazpacho and orzo salad, Richard declared that Brandon is his hero. "The bet wasn't really about lunch," he said (while reminding the Lowitzes that this particular lunch didn't count toward their total, then making a side bet that Brandon would not go scuba diving once each week while in Bali). "The bet was about trying to rise above the pressures of New York."

The six months since the wager marked the passage to a new era, he explained. "That was a time when things were still running at full throttle," he said of the galloping economy of the past decade. "But since then," he continued, "the country has taken a sharp turn. All around us people are looking at the insanity of the past few years and taking a step back. In that way, Brandon is emblematic of what drives our world."

As to who actually won the bet—Richard, Jill, and Brandon left it to me to decide. I took the job seriously. Richard's larger reason for making the bet, I reasoned, was to prove that life is so overloaded that it is impossible to find four hours a month for lunch. In that he was right. If the Lowitzes had stayed at their jobs, they would never have met the twenty-four-lunch goal.

The reason the Lowitzes tried the impossible in the first place, however, was to prove that they could defy the odds, break the rules, and put their life ahead of their work. Their trip to Bali was certainly doing all that. And since they would spend every day together for the next three months, they could potentially present Richard with enough receipts to cover the cost of their trip.

But this bet was never really about the money; it was a quirky affirmation of priorities. My verdict, therefore, was that it be settled not with dollars but with time. Those cooking classes the Lowitzes are taking? They owe Richard (and me!) an exotic, leisurely meal when they return home.

BRIEFCASES

The constant, scolding ache in my right shoulder, I am somewhat relieved to report, is not a new symptom of age, nor is it anything that will require surgery. It's my shoulder bag.

Specifically, it's the sleek, sexy laptop I carry in that bag, a laptop I chose because it weighs so little—only 2.9 pounds. Of course, that doesn't count the spare battery, which weighs nearly a pound but gives me four extra hours of mobile work time. And it doesn't count the A/C charger that I bring along whenever I travel, just in case (heaven forbid) I use up those four extra hours. Or the notes (file folders, steno pads, documents) that are the raw material for what eventually goes on the computer screen.

I weighed it all the other day. My lightweight laptop, with its case and its baggage, means I'm lugging an extra thirteen pounds.

I'm hardly the only one who's carrying the weight of the work on her shoulder. Any morning, on any train platform, there are dozens of bags that make mine look underfed.

Waiting for the 7:29 to Grand Central one rush hour I got to talking to a woman named Lisa Chung whose shoulder sagged under a bulging leather case that held not just her ThinkPad, but also her Portege. Two laptops, plus her office pumps, plus a doorstop-sized book she was reading for an after-hours leadership seminar. All told, she guessed the combined weight to be "about ten pounds?"

On the moon, maybe. Let's just say that my relative sense of weight is based on the twenty-pound barbells at the gym (no, I don't actually *use* them, but I have put them back onto the rack occasionally), and this was *much* heavier. "It's my exercise for the day," she said with a shrug (which probably hurt, given what she was holding). "That, and running for the train."

The more revealing question, however, is not how much are we carrying, but why on earth are we carrying it? The simplest answer is that we have more work to do. So much more that we can't possibly do it during the confines of a traditional (remember what that is?) workday, so we have to do it at home. And on the way home. And on the way back to work again. The corollary to this is that we've shaped our world so that we can work anywhere—which also means we have no excuse not to work *everywhere.*

True. But then why are so many people with overstuffed briefcases not actually working? Look at them. They're reading the newspaper (a practice I clearly applaud) or napping or chatting on cell phones. I have been known to get on a two-hour flight carrying my laptop and a breezy five-hundred-page document I need to read for background research. Somehow I never get around to glancing at the document or starting up the machine. I do, however, manage to plow through the stack of glossy (and very thick) magazines I've bought right before boarding.

Psychiatrists have theories about us. Dr. Alan Manevitz, who drags his own briefcase to New York–Presbyterian Hospital every day, says our briefcase has become our "transitional object," something we cart around because it makes us feel secure. Like an eight-year-old boy who would happily cart his Pokémon collection back and forth to school, even though his teacher forbids him from taking it out of his backpack.

Back on my train platform, a few feet from where Lisa Chung was bench-pressing her laptops, Hartley Konnett was a chain-smoking example of this hypothesis, sneaking in one last cigarette before his trip to the trading floor. At his feet was his briefcase, which he said "goes under my desk, where it sits all day until I carry it back home, where it sits all night." He's tried to leave the thing at work, he said, but "you come into the office without it and you feel naked. People actually comment."

Dr. David Yamins, who never leaves his office at Maimonides Medical Center without packing prescription pads, journal articles, and his computer, and who spends his daily commute listening to tapes of psychiatry residents and their patients, says this need to work isn't necessarily a bad thing. "We're getting an awful lot done," he says. "What's wrong with that?"

But I'm not so sure. I can still see my grandmother on a five-hour flight we took together when I was thirteen. An avid reader (she's the one who was still taking courses in subjects like Chinese history in her eighties), she didn't open a book or even plan her itinerary. Instead, we talked. On train rides, she looked out the window.

My grandmother knew how to sit and watch. Now my generation has improved the world so much that we don't remember how. As an experiment, I rode the train into work empty-handed one morning, save for my wallet. I lasted twelve minutes. Then I gave in and began to scribble a to-do list on the back flap of my checkbook.

SICK AT WORK

Many years ago, during a violent winter flu season, I had an interview scheduled in Maine with the state's attorney general. I also had a wicked cold. But I was a spanking-new reporter then, terrified at the thought of missing a deadline, so I swallowed a variety of over-the-counter promises, snorted too much nasal spray, and boarded a very small commuter plane.

By the time I landed in Augusta, my ears were so stuffed that everything echoed and the ground shifted and rolled when I walked. I arrived, on schedule, at the statehouse. Then, just as promptly, I passed out. I conducted the interview while lying on a couch, sipping tea. When the attorney general said his good-byes, he suggested—quite kindly, considering the circumstances—that next time I should "please just stay home."

Judging from the people who are hacking and sneezing each year come flu time, it is advice not easily followed. Why *don't* we just stay home?

"I tried," said Rita, my hairdresser, who worked the week

before Christmas one year despite aching muscles and a headache so fierce she squinted while she snipped. "I called and told them I wasn't coming in and they said yes, I was; there were clients."

"I should," said Dr. Stuart Lewis, a medical school professor, who admits to coming to work feeling lousy because his patients depend on him to send *them* home to bed. "My wife is always asking me the same question," he said with a laugh. "And I have to explain it's because I'm totally indispensable."

The good doctor tells his patients to call in sick when they have a fever (meaning they are most likely to be contagious) or if they feel too ill to concentrate on their work. Staying home won't make you any better, he explained, but it will make you more comfortable. And, as the attorney general of Maine made clear, it will keep everyone else at the office from catching what you've got. Bringing a virus to work allows that virus to get down to work. Germs "are very efficient at going from one person to the next," Stuart said. "That's what they do for a living."

He gives this advice knowing it will be ignored, just as he so often ignores it himself. "People drag themselves to work feeling lousy because it's much harder to be at home than at work," he said. A day at home is divided between soap operas you aren't able to follow and thoughts of all the work you aren't getting done. Better to hoard those sick days for a return of the plague, or, even worse, a day when your child is too sick to go to school.

Sick kids. Ahhh. Now, there's a whole other can of germs. Just ask Mrs. Klein, our school nurse. More than once my son's sore throat, which I'd hoped was nothing when he woke up, blossomed into an unmistakable something by lunchtime. When I apologized for sending him in the first place, Mrs. Klein just laughed. "I've gotten notes that say, 'She was throwing up all night—but she seems better now,' " she said. With two sons of her own, she tries to be understanding. "No one has time for their kids to be sick. They have meetings. They have places to be. They need their kids to be in school."

I should note that Mrs. Klein had a cold on the day we spoke, but she came to work anyway because she knew it was hard to find a substitute nurse. She is very careful, she said, to wash her hands constantly. But kids can't be counted on to wash their hands. They can, bless them, be counted on to sneeze on their best friend's snack. And those very efficient germs can be counted on to travel from friend to parent, who then goes off to work and sneezes on the rest of us.

If I sound a little cranky it's because, as I write this, I'm not feeling all that hot myself. My throat now has the unmistakable warning tickle, and my nose is starting to run. I managed to oh-so-casually mention this to all the doctors I spoke to in the paragraphs above, but none of them was terribly impressed and none had a miracle cure. Sounds like a cold, they said. Stay home if you run a fever and just let it run its course.

"I'm very glad," added Dr. Jonathan Jacobs, an infectious disease specialist at New York Weill Cornell Medical College, "that we're not doing this interview in person."

THE CHILD IS
THE FATHER OF MAN

Who made the last dozen calls to your pager or cell phone? Is your boss on the list? The baby-sitter? The carry-out place on the corner? Added together, these numbers likely form a mosaic of your life.

Now scroll with me through the calls to Joan Jaffe's cell phone—a phone she bought as a link to her ailing ninety-one-year-old mother. Added together, such numbers will one day form the mosaic of each of our lives.

Joan, a travel agent near Chicago, is one of seven million of us who will care for elderly relatives this year. And her worries—our worries—are reshaping the world. "Demand for elder care is growing faster than the demand for child care or school-age care," said Barry Wanger, a spokesman for the American Business Collaboration for Quality Dependent Care, a coalition of seventeen major corporations that have spent $100 million over the years to improve the quality of such care in nearly seventy communities.

On the day he told me this, his own mother was moving into a nursing home; he apologized for being distracted. "It's something everyone will go through," he said, adding that employers who have not quite gotten the knack of helping employees through the shoals of child care "are just starting to figure this one out."

The first thing they learn—the first thing each of us will learn—is that this is different than child care. "With a child, a healthy child, you can plan," said Carol House from Cutchogue, New York, whose seventy-five-year-old mother had lung cancer, heart disease, and a stroke. "You know when you're going to have the baby. You know that when that baby is five he'll go to kindergarten and by the time he's sixteen he won't be home as much as you are. With a parent it can come out of the blue, and you can't promise an employer 'I'll be back in six weeks.' "

And even if you are back at work, there's a good chance you won't really be concentrating on your job. The infrastructure of elder care is both more complex and less complete than that of child care, said Pat Netsch of San Francisco, whose eighty-six-year-old mother, paralyzed on one side by a stroke, lived with her for months before she reluctantly moved into an assisted-care facility. "Medicare, Social Security, home care," Pat said. "You have to do that during work hours. You can't do it at home. You can't do it on weekends."

But the biggest difference, the most overwhelming difference, has nothing to do with logistics. Caring for a healthy child is about happiness and hope. Caring for a failing parent is about mourning and loss. Caring for a child is about living for the future. Caring for a parent is about living in the moment.

"Once again, I have become a parent," said Margaret Tierney, who has two grown children. This time, though, the "child" was her ninety-one-year-old father, who moved into Margaret's Suwannee, Georgia, home but often did not know where he was or who his daughter was. Instead of 2 A.M. feedings, she said, she was roused in the middle of the night to find her father waiting at the door for a phantom guest or wandering the yard searching, inexplicably, for cans of gasoline. "My babies," is how she described her father and her ninety-year-old mother, who also lived with her and was crippled with arthritis. "My friends will ask me, 'How are your babies?' "

And isn't that our ultimate fear? That inevitably we will become the parents where we used to be the children? It is a reversal of roles that, in its own way, is sadder than death. I watched my mother care for my grandmother, who lost her vision suddenly on a frigid Christmas morning. When she was diagnosed with cancer, she refused to go back to the hospital, and her two daughters took turns at her bedside honoring that last wish. And I've had the briefest glimpse of my own possible future when my father went for major heart surgery several years ago. Their job was to worry about us. Now it's our job to worry about them.

To take better care of her "babies," Margaret Tierney, a manager for AT&T, began to telecommute from home. At the time I interviewed her, she had not taken a vacation for two years. Pat Netsch turned down a job promotion at Chevron that would have required frequent travel. Carol House, a veterinary microbiologist, stopped working altogether, retiring at age fifty-five.

Joan Jaffe kept her travel agency job. "Going to work was a godsend to me," she said, "to go there and do something productive." But she reordered her life for her mother in so many other ways, helping the elderly woman stay in her own home, surrounded by twenty-four-hour nursing care, during her long battle with lung cancer. The cell phone was the bridge between that home and Joan's office. "She's really the only one who had the number," she said. And in the final months, when the illness created delusion and panic, there were frequent, frantic calls resulting in white-knuckle dashes, usually in rush-hour traffic.

Joan's mother died several weeks after we first spoke. When Joan went back to work, her cell phone went along, too. She powered it on and placed it within reach, though she knew there was no one likely to call.

CRYING AT WORK

The Internet boom busted during the years I've been watching the workplace, and I heard tell of one burly CEO—whose once-vibrant company faced the layoffs of hundreds of workers—who sat in an empty conference room and cried.

Fashion magazines, too, played musical chairs with its editors as a regular diversion, and gossip spread that one of those left chairless—a woman whose very existence was about keeping up appearances—locked her door and cried as she cleaned out her desk.

The saying goes, Never let them see you sweat. But in today's macho workplace we don't mind sweat. It's tears we can't handle. Work is the vessel into which we pour so much of ourselves—hope and disappointment, elation and rage, satisfaction and frustration. Yet any damp display of these emotions is seen as weakness. "Do anything you can," said career consultant Marjorie Brody, "to keep from crying at work."

I admit I am a workplace crier. When I was chewed out by

my first editor for a misattributed quote, I cried. When a story I thought was destined for the front page didn't make it, I cried. When I was scooped on an article I'd been researching for months, I cried hard. Most of these crying jags were short, but one went on and on. I returned from maternity leave and cried every day for at least a month, lost in a sodden fog of exhaustion.

No matter how much I've cried, however, no one at work (at least not that I know of) ever saw me do it. Newsrooms don't have the luxury of doors (at best they have very public cubicles), and disappearing to the ladies' room was not an option because so many of my editors (an unforeseen downside of progress?) were women. Instead I held myself together long enough to flee the building, then walked round and round the block, sunglasses on even in the rain, whimpering into a Kleenex.

There was a pretzel vendor in Times Square who probably wondered about my sanity, but I decided that was better than my bosses wondering about my stability. Tears can paralyze a workplace. Cass Bruton-Ward once managed an employee who cried at the slightest criticism. She was also reduced to tears by minor glitches. "If someone inadvertently left company letterhead in the laser printer, making her have to reprint her two- or three-page document," Cass said, "she would sometimes launch into a tearful tantrum."

An occasional crier herself (but only behind closed doors), Cass understood that some people just can't help it. "You can't just tell such a person don't cry. It doesn't work," she said. "It's not unlike stuttering or having a facial tic." But that said, you also can't just have that person bawling at the photocopy machine. It took the intervention of a psychologist to get this employee's emotions under control.

Julie Swensen agreed that some tears can't be stopped. I met her six months after her fiancé left a message on her office voice mail breaking their engagement, and she was still crying. Her personal sorrow seeped into her work because her ex's father was the largest client of her Minneapolis public relations firm. Whenever his name came up in a meeting, she found herself weeping. This despite months of therapy and a prescription for Zoloft.

"People have been very understanding—women, that is," she said, adding that "men get totally freaked out by that kind of emotion in the workplace." In an ideal world they would see her tears for what they are, she argued. "We all have emotions, and they come to work with us every day."

Marjorie Brody, co-author of *Help! Was That a Career Limiting Move?*, was alarmed when I told her Julie's story. "I hate to sound unsympathetic," she said of all that sobbing, "but she really might be better off staying away from her business for a while. She's going to lose her employees."

Julie begged to differ. Her employees, she said, her voice filling with tears, are what kept her going. Her assistant "can tell from the tone of my voice what my mood is, and when I sound like I'm going to cry, she comes into my office and shuts the internal blinds so no one else can see. Then she shuts the door and guards it for a while."

STRESS AND CHOCOLATE

A few facts to make you feel calm and relaxed as you leisurely sip your morning coffee:

Nearly a quarter of all American workers have been driven to tears by the stress of work. Nearly half describe their office as a place of "verbal abuse and yelling," and one-third admit to doing some of that yelling themselves. One in eight of us has called in sick because we were too stressed out to work, and one in five of us has up and quit. Thirty percent say their work is filled with "unreasonable deadlines," and 52 percent have logged twelve-hour workdays to get the job done. Half of us routinely skip lunch. A third of us find ourselves too stressed to sleep. Sixty-two percent end the workday with neck pain, 44 percent with strained eyes, and 38 percent with aching hands. One in twelve complain that their desk chair "hurts my butt."

All right, okay, *enough* with the statistics. We already know that we are stressed. What, then, are we supposed to *do* about it?

It may relieve you (but not necessarily relax you) to know that a lot of people are spending a lot of energy trying to help. The same decade that spawned all this tension—bringing us the dubious benefits of E-mail and wireless messaging and instant, constant conversation—has also bred job categories devoted to helping us cope. Magnet Communications, for instance, has a director of stress management (yep, that's what it says on his business cards), and the position is occupied by a white Maltese dog named Merlin who belongs to the CEO.

At CooperKatz and Company a human being is in charge of stress management, and media director Andrea Katz lights aromatherapy candles in conference rooms, plays New Age music on the stereo, and administers "hug therapy" to anyone having a bad day. At ArsDigita, a Massachusetts software creator, there is a piano in the lobby for employees to play. And at Delta Dental Plan, a Michigan insurer, workers are given little white flags. During a frustrating sales call, the white flag is literally waved, and co-workers know to be nice to (or steer clear of) the harried employee.

Where do companies get these ideas? Probably from a crush of books written by seemingly serene people who simply cannot be nearly as calm as they sound because—and I speak from experience here—book writing means deadlines and revisions, and arguments with editors, and a summer vacation spent watching your children pad off to the beach with your husband while you are left behind to pound away on a rewrite of chapter 3.

Let me pause for a moment to take a deep breath. The experts talk a lot about taking deep breaths. I always thought it was the oxygenated equivalent of counting to ten, ensuring that I pause before I do something rash. But Dr. Bill Crawford, author of *All Stressed Up & Nowhere to Go!,* explains that breathing is not about restraint but about control. The pace of your breathing, he says, is something you have control over, even when everything else is falling apart.

The next step, the good doctor says, is to chant the word "relax" when you exhale, to loosen up the muscles that have tightened in your shoulders and your neck (but never, unfortunately, in your abs or your gluts, which might make this stress worth it). While chanting, ask yourself, "How would I rather be feeling?" then envision a time when you felt that way and play the memory like a movie in your head. Our bodies respond chemically to our thoughts, the best example being a sexual fantasy. "You know it isn't happening, but your body responds as if it were," he explains.

To paraphrase Descartes, "I think I'm relaxed, therefore I am."

Barbara Bailey Reinhold, author of *Toxic Work: How to Overcome Stress, Overload, Burnout and Revitalize Your Career,* takes all this imagining a step further. Instead of just thinking about lovely things, she wants you to do them. Her strategy includes making a list of twenty small, instantly gratifying acts that make you feel better, such as telling a joke to a colleague, putting fresh flowers on your desk, taking a walk or a hot bath, or romping with the dog. Keep copies wherever you might need them, so when you find yourself on the brink, you have "an emotional apothecary from which you can extract an ameliorative suggestion or two."

I've made my list: read vacation brochures, call Mimi,

have a manicure . . . I'm practicing my breathing (the last time I practiced breathing, however, I asked for an epidural anyway). But I've also mined another nugget from all this data. Stress drives 26 percent of us to consume chocolate. The pollsters describe this as a problem. I like to think of it as a solution.

BRINGING WORK

BACK HOME

GOING HOME AGAIN

I tried. I really did. I got up every morning, kissed little cheeks, left lists for the baby-sitter, and headed for the train. But before I even found a spot at the station parking lot I felt my stress barometer rising.

So I tried something else. I started skipping the train and driving to work instead, an improvement, I reasoned, because I wouldn't have to operate on someone else's schedule. But because a lot of other people in the New York metropolitan area had the same idea, I battled mind-numbing traffic.

I bought books on tape.

I tried commuting at different hours.

I listened to NPR.

I changed baby-sitters.

I changed my diet to one that promised I'd have more energy.

I changed my wardrobe so that I'd feel less confined and more comfortable.

I stopped at Starbucks on the way home to decompress.

I drove the boys to school myself so I would have more time with them.

I tried and tried and tried and tried. But I kept having that dream where I ran down empty alleyways in the fog, never finding my unspecified destination. More accurately, I had that dream only on nights when I managed to get to REM sleep. It's probably not a coincidence that *tried* and *tired* are two words rooted in the same letters.

There was no single cymbals-and-drumroll moment when I decided to move my work back home. Like all the other major changes I'd made over the years, it was less a decision and more a matter of gravitational pull. I was not yet covering the workplace when I did this, but I was an early example of what would soon become a full-blown trend. I began as a telecommuter, a grateful beneficiary of the technology revolution that began with my first clunky cell phone. Eventually I became a SOHO—industry shorthand for "small office/home office"—a reflection of the as yet incomplete societal revolution that says our quality of life matters at least as much as our success at work. I inched my way from one to the next slowly. I started by working from home one day a week, then two, then as often as I could get away with it.

Eventually I cut the cord entirely and gave up my job at the *Times*. Like the first time I quit (to follow Bruce to Texas), this sounds much braver than it actually was. I kept writing for the paper, first as a regular contributor to *The New York Times Magazine* and later as the scribbler of the Life's Work column.

If you'd asked me back then why I did this, I would have said it was because of the children. They were getting older and I could already see that I would be needed at home more as they grew, not less. The bigger the children, the bigger the problems, Grandma used to say. I worried about being away from them when they were babies, but I came to realize that the loss was mine more than theirs. A baby-sitter can kiss a boo-boo. But what surrogate can make it better when they come home to report that the school bully has set his sights on them, or that the big kid down the street has offered them drugs, or that their best friend has a new best friend, which means they will never have any friends ever again?

The welfare of my children was my stated reason for leaving, but it was not my only reason. I also did this for me. I learned during those days I worked at home that I work better that way. The home-office life won't fit every job or suit every personality, but I found that I was more creative, more productive, and (relatively) more disciplined (we'll get to that in a few chapters) when I was the boss.

I launched my new life by accumulating all the necessary technology: a new computer, printer, and fax, and a very complicated and not entirely dependable voice-mail system. In the years since then I've also acquired tools I never expected to need. Like the OPEN/CLOSED sign over my desk that I flip back and forth to let the boys know whether I am free to talk or too busy to be disturbed. Or the portable heater in the corner (along with a new electrical outlet), because who knew that this was the coldest room in the house? My initial home office plans didn't include a pile of dog toys either, but workplaces evolve with circumstance.

By moving work back home, I gained everything I'd hoped I would gain—the freedom to set my own hours, to turn down assignments, to be home when I needed or wanted to be—but I also lost things I still miss. The office telephone line, for instance, where the charges went directly to the metro desk and I never had to spend hours with a calculator figuring out which call went with which article and who to invoice for what. I miss the reassurance of a salaried paycheck, too, and my employer's contribution to my Social Security and Medicare taxes. I miss the ability to keep work at a physical distance from home, and I really miss the camaraderie of the newsroom during the many, lengthy pauses between spurts of work. That's partly why my phone bill is so high: I spend far too much time talking to the friends I used to meet in the elevator.

Once in a while, when they've had a trying day, some of those colleagues tell me they wish they were at home. And once in a while, especially when adrenaline-pumping news is breaking and the newsroom is crackling with energy and purpose, I tell them I wish I were at work. If there's a theme to this entire book, that's it. My own life's choices don't represent a solution, because no choice is a solution so much as a new packet of complications.

There's a fable I learned in childhood. I'm not sure of its origins, so let's credit the squirrelly Belkins from Russia. Everyone in the world, the story goes, puts his shoes in one big pile and then each person gets a turn to choose any pair from the pile as their own. They each have a chance to slip into shoes that are fancier or shinier, but, according to the fable, they all wind up with the shoes they brought because that's what fits them best. What's true for shoes is true for so many of the choices in our lives. Whatever we choose will have its share of scuff marks and holes. But they will be our scuff marks, our holes, the ones that come to fit us best.

LIFE IS A SWIVEL CHAIR

I hear them before I see them—the eleven-year-old followed by the eight-year-old—as they clomp up the stairs that lead to my office. They knock (when they remember), then in they come, dropping their backpacks at my feet like an offering. If I'm on the phone they do their best to be quiet, which means they shush loudly at each other until I hang up. When I'm finally theirs, they fill my lap with a jumble of artwork and homework and memos from the PTA. I give hugs and praise and savor whatever nuggets they offer up about their day. All this serves to postpone, but never prevent, the final part of the ritual. The part where I notice the time, tell them I love them, then boot them out the door.

Being a working parent means having at least one moment of the day when you push your children away. Because guilt is an equal-opportunity companion, there is a version of that moment to suit any frenetic schedule: early in the morning, when you tiptoe out before they even wake up; during the late-day phone call home, a call you really don't have time for because your four o'clock meeting has begun;

between dinner and bedtime (assuming you made it home for either) when you have to read a hefty brief instead of *Harry Potter.*

And then there are the business trips—the mother lodes (parent lodes?) of conflicted moments. I was quite the sight in the Philippines a few winters ago, wandering among ramshackle jungle huts in search of a phone because it was eight o'clock in New York and I'd promised to call in time to say good night. (I never did find one. I did penance with extra presents.) I topped that during one ugly moment in the Atlanta airport when the airline gave away my seat on the last flight out, meaning I would not be home when my children woke up on Thanksgiving morning. (I threatened to walk through the security door to board the plane anyway; a seat was somehow found for me on another carrier.)

When I traded my life as a commuter for one as a SOHO I smugly thought I had eliminated all the "moments." I could be at work and be at home at the same time. Evan was giddy that first morning. Wow. He had his baby-sitter *and* his mommy. But when I glided off to my desk, coffee mug in hand, he was outraged. How to explain that I was his—but only sometimes. That I was there—but also out of reach. He stood and cried on his side of the office door. I stood and cried on mine.

Fact is, we *can't* be fully at home and fully at work at the same time—not if work is in a newsroom in Times Square and not even if work is in the next room. Work and life don't overlap so much as they collide or intersect, leaving us to sit in our ergonomically correct swivel chairs and pivot between the two. And each time we turn toward one, we are, in that moment, turning away from the other.

My moment now comes most often at 3:15 in the afternoon when my boys rocket into my office. By 3:30 they have to leave. I have to work. I can't change that, but I can change what I tell them about it. For years I apologized: "I'd rather be with you, but if I don't write there won't be money for toys." Then one morning I found Alex perched in his booster seat, scribbling furiously with a pencil on a yellow legal pad. I asked what he wanted for breakfast and he shooed me away. "I can't talk, Mommy," he growled. "If I don't finish my article, my editor will be mad with me."

My message, I saw, had been that work was a mix of fear and drudgery, a nasty thing designed only to keep me away from them. And while there are times when all those things are true, bleak and desperate are not at the core of how I feel about my work and not how I hope my sons will one day feel about their own. I work because I have to. I do this particular *kind* of work because I choose to. I realize that makes me lucky, and that is the point—I want them to see the luck, the fulfillment, the fun.

I still show them the door, but I do it differently. Or I try to. On deadline days I can, I confess, be heard to threaten that there will be no more food, clothing, shelter, or Nintendo—ever—unless they let me write. But in saner times I ask about their day, then tell them about mine. About my latest magazine assignment. Or about my column, which might even mention them once in a while. I use words like *exciting* and *interesting,* and I promise them all the details, but not until later. Not until the moment I turn off the computer, swivel that chair back around, and finish working—at least until *after* they go to bed.

TRYING TO CONNECT

For more than six months my SOHO life was stalled on the entrance ramp to the information superhighway. Being a cutting-edge, technologically savvy worker, I signed up for my very own digital subscriber line, or DSL, an Internet connection so fast that it left last century's must-have, the 56K modem, in the dust. At least that's what the ads said. Let's put it this way: I just hope it's faster than the companies that supply it.

The arc of all technology is from indulgent to indispensable. In between there is an interminable moment when everyone must have "it" but not everyone can get "it," where the potential gets bogged down by the infrastructure. That's why we all listened to endless busy signals on AOL in its infancy. And now that we've all become more computer dependent—spoiled by ISDN lines and T1 lines at the office and impatient to bring that speed home—that's why so many of us have war stories to tell about the wait for DSL.

When I first sent Flashcom my deposit they told me that due to high demand, my installation would be scheduled in six to eight weeks. The visit would not be from Flashcom, but Northpoint, because, in this complicated DSL world, it takes three separate companies to install any one line. So I waited two months, only to learn that the wires to my house were not up to grade.

It seems this happens a lot. On average, 40 percent of would-be customers, whose computers are within proper range of a DSL-equipped central telephone office, run into wiring complications. I learned this from a very nice executive way up the management ladder at Flashcom (who preferred not to use his name here in print because the company was—natch—in the midst of going public. He also directed me to a Web site, www.DSLreports.com, one of a number of sites that have sprung up for trading gripes about DSL providers across the country. It made me feel much less alone).

But I'm getting ahead of my story. Flashcom sent a "trouble ticket" to what, way back then, was still Bell Atlantic. They were the third company in this dance, because they owned the actual wires. Although I never saw any evidence that Bell Atlantic had been to my home, I received an E-mail weeks later saying that the problem had been fixed and that I was scheduled for a two-hour appointment—with Northpoint again—to install a lot of hardware through my walls and onto my computer. When the very nice technician was finished, my desk was decorated with a pretty DSL modem. Unfortunately, the lights on the modem, which were supposed to turn green, stayed red and orange instead.

Bell Atlantic had never fixed the wires. Another "trouble ticket" was sent and then Flashcom and I spent several months exchanging E-mails. Theirs were upbeat and peppy, saying that my outside wiring was now complete and it was time for my inside wiring! Mine were less than upbeat, saying that no, the inside wiring had already been installed, but the outside wiring was still a problem.

Meanwhile, Bell Atlantic became Verizon, went on strike, settled, and bought a 55-percent stake in Northpoint. The only thing they didn't do was fix my wires. I, on the other hand, decided to give up, get back my deposit, and remain in the Stone Age. But I wouldn't go out quietly. So I put on my reporter's hat, called Verizon and Flashcom, and asked them to comment, for the record, on why it takes more than six months to get DSL service.

Both companies agreed they are having growing pains. The entire industry is only two years old, explained the Flashcom executive (who didn't have DSL at his own house because he did not want to go to the trouble of getting his subpar inside wiring replaced). Joan Rassmussen, of the public relations department at Verizon, compared this to the early days of electricity, when homeowners kept their gas lamps installed because the newfangled electric wires so often failed.

It might have been coincidence, but within twenty-four hours of my call there was a very nice Verizon technician on the pole outside my house. (A technician, by the way, who had given up on getting DSL for his own house after waiting three months.) By the end of the day the lights on my modem had turned green, and it was left to me to make a few small adjustments to my computer. These didn't make my DSL work, but they did disable my existing dial-up modem, leaving me with no Internet connection at all.

That led to a visit from an exceedingly nice Northpoint

technician who hunkered down for two hours in my office. When he emerged he declared that my DSL modem worked when connected to his laptop, which meant the problem was with my computer and could probably be solved if I purchased a new Ethernet card. While I was out I stopped at the hardware store and looked for a new gas lantern, just in case.

FRIENDS AT WORK

One evening Bruce came home with the news that he was losing his best buddy at work. Bob was off to new adventures, and when he left, an important beat in the rhythm of Bruce's day would leave, too. Workplace friendships are a crossbreed of the species, sturdy yet fragile at the same time. They start out as lunch and evolve into loyalty. As Laura Senturia, a publicist in Waltham, Massachusetts, told me about her buddy Marybeth McLean Roberts: "Somewhere along the way, 'Marybeth-from-work' became simply 'Marybeth.' "

It's a transition that comes with a lot of warning labels. There are small land mines to worry about, such as what to do when your best friend gets *your* promotion, and the more prosaic risk, that you become one of those people who talk about nothing but shop over what is supposed to be a social dinner. "It's like an office romance without the romance," joked Karen Wright, who worked in fund-raising at Minnesota State University with her close friend Ann Rosenquist Fee. The two women sang together in a folk band after hours. On top of that, Ann's husband and Karen's significant other were professors together at the same university (which is how Karen began dating him in the first place).

These multiple ties were tested when Karen was appointed chair of a search committee and Ann applied for the job. The two women dealt with the potential strain on their friendship "by just not talking about it," Ann said, even though she was itching to know who else was being considered for the position and what her chances were. Karen, for her part, bent over backward to prove her impartiality, even though "I thought Ann was qualified in every way." The story has a happy ending: Ann got the job and Karen became her boss.

The daily stresses of an office can strain a friendship, but I think the truest test is when you take the office away. What happens, in other words, when "Marybeth-is-no-longer-at-work"? Laura and Marybeth found that out when Marybeth got married and moved to Chicago. She and Laura, who used to spend twelve hours a day together, were now linked by morning E-mails and weekly phone calls.

Friendships are really life's best souvenirs; you keep a few from high school, a few from college, a handful from summer camp. My own core group of friends, the ones who shaped my sense of self, then staked a lifelong claim on it, were gathered during my first few years of work. We were all *New York Times* clerks back then, answering reporters' phones (in a world before voice mail) and dreaming of the day when someone else would answer ours. We spent most of our nights and weekends at the office, but during our free time we would gather in one of our tiny apartments, where we'd order takeout and trade gossip over who was likely to be promoted to reporter first. If we were as successful as we hoped to be, we wouldn't all work in the same city again for a very long time.

As we'd predicted, the work that brought us together began to tease us apart. Moscow, Beijing, Tokyo, even Houston and Seattle are very far away, and while the bonds don't break, they change with distance and with time. When I was still writing from the newsroom, one of the closest friends I am ever likely to have asked me to guard the door while she ducked into the office bathroom and took a pregnancy test. Fast-forward a few years, after work had taken us to separate places, and she became pregnant again. I learned about that baby through the grapevine.

The trick, then, is keeping "simply Marybeth" from becoming "Marybeth-who-was-once-my-friend." Laura and Marybeth vowed to do just that, and they planned a girls' night out in Chicago whenever they both could clear a weekend for a visit. Bruce and Bob, in turn, still see each other often because his wife and I (who have become a whole separate category of friends) see to it that they do. And me, well, the week of Bob's send-off party, I called my own Marybeth and invited her (and her little girl) to lunch.

GETTING ORGANIZED

Back when I worked in what my children call a "real office," my workspace was relatively neat. Not compulsively so, mind you, but organized enough that I could find most things eventually. Home, on the other hand, was always more of a challenge. I like to describe the place as "informal" or "lived in." Translated that means "the boys' snow boots are still scattered in the front hallway come July."

When I moved my career from a real office to a home office I'd hoped that my comparatively orderly work habits would somehow permeate the rest of the house. Have you ever heard the tale of the magic geranium? (This is the last of Grandma's fables. I promise.) A woman living in misery and squalor is given an enchanted flower by a wise man who tells her to take it home where it will transform her life. She sets it on the table as instructed, but sees that its crimson beauty makes the linens look shabby, so she scrubs them. Then she notices how her newly washed linens make her floor seem dull, so she scrubs it, too. Eventually her entire home is sparkling.

Well, plants have never stood a chance at our house, so it probably won't surprise you to hear that the spell can also work its magic in reverse. Over time, my office came to look "lived in" as well. My file cabinets bulged with notes I had not glanced at in five years. Folders that didn't fit into those cabinets were stacked in piles on the floor. The pullout couch became a storage area and was so covered with books and papers that barely a patch of upholstery was left showing.

One particularly bad day a certain notepad became lost in this void—a pad that contained pages of notes for this book. Hours of searching finally unearthed not only the notepad (it was still in an inside pocket of a suitcase I had taken on a recent trip) but also the business card of one Sande Nelson, whose name had been given to me months earlier by a concerned friend.

Sande is a professional organizer, a profession growing almost as fast as the clutter in American offices. The National Association of Professional Organizers, which had 57 members at its founding conference in 1987, now has 1,358 members, divided into such subspecialties as Collections/Memorabilia/Photographs, Goal Setting, Garages/Attics/Basements, Filing Systems, Time Management, and, my personal favorite, Work with Chronically Disorganized.

K. J. McCorry, the spokesperson for the association and owner of Officiency, Inc., which is based in Denver, talks in the efficient tones of her profession. "You need to find a place for everything," she said, "then put everything in its place." Trying to make me feel less like a slob and more like a trend, she told me that workplaces are ever more disorganized because workers have more to keep track of—more E-mail, more computer printouts, more data. "People who used to be organized are now feeling very overwhelmed, very disorganized, and they're not sure why," she said.

Ninety percent of her clients, she estimated, used to have things under control. (The other 10 percent, I assume, are the types who store their snow boots in the hallway.)

Those who have hired professional organizers say they are as magic as any geranium. "I have a filing system now," cooed Maria Vega, a Manhattan electrologist who hired Get Organized! (Sande's company) to help her move from one office to another. "I never used to have a filing system. I used to have a pile."

Coveting a system of my own, I called Sande, who came to my house for my initial consultation. Wearing royal blue–tinted glasses and carrying two huge shoulder bags filled with "stuff," she cleared a space for herself on my couch, then rummaged through one satchel for a bottle of seltzer. "I live on planet earth," she said, following my gaze as I took in the jumble of empty lunch containers and seemingly random file folders she was returning to her bag. "No one can be perfect. Everyone makes a mess sometimes. But life should have an underlying sense of order." Then she asked me a lot of questions, provided no immediate answers, said I was not a hopeless case, and promised to return in a few weeks with a custom-made game plan telling me everything from how to label my files to which office supplies to buy. (I'll let you know how it goes.)

Two days after our meeting, I discovered she'd left one of her many files behind. I cleared a spot of honor for that folder and the space looked so nice that I went on to clear off the entire couch. This made my desk look messier than usual, so I started to clear that, too. By the time Sande returned, I figured, I might even have space for a sassy red plant in the corner.

(LACK OF) EXERCISE

Once upon a time I was in pretty good shape. That was back when I would head for the gym after work at least three times a week. That was also before I had children. In the decade since then I have been on a constant quest to fit exercise into the crevice between my life and my work. Of course, if I exercised more, it might not be such a tight squeeze.

I know that other people manage to work and work out. It's just that they seem to do it in ways that don't work for me. There's the first-thing-in-the-morning approach, but as much as I would *love* to get up at dawn, I am crushed to have to say that my husband leaves for work at 5 A.M., which means our young sons would be home alone if I left for the gym, a situation frowned upon by the bureau of child welfare. There's the after-the-kids-are-asleep approach, but lately the boys seem to go to bed later than I do.

There's also the exercise-while-commuting approach. Paul Clarke, a consultant with Magnet Communications in Chicago, ran home twenty miles once a week while training for a marathon. Jason Rok, a stock trader in Manhattan, bikes five miles to the office every day at 5:30 A.M. But my office is seven steps from my bedroom, so no matter how fast the run, I wouldn't expend the calories found in your average Oreo. (Yes, I could stop eating Oreos, but anyone who would suggest that has obviously never worked at home, steps away from the kitchen.)

Some buff folks create a gym at home, on the theory that this eliminates excuses. "I put it where I can trip over it," said Pat Fiore, president of her own public relations firm. "Sort of like the milk being in the back of the supermarket, and you have to go past all the good stuff to get it, only in this case I have to go past the workout equipment to get to my beloved books and TV." I've learned I am impervious to such guilt. I own a stair machine, which sits in my office, where I stare at it all day. It is usually draped with a dog leash and a coat. Why, you ask, don't I use that machine in the mornings, during the hours when I cannot leave the house for the gym? I would, but the noise would wake the children and the dog.

Pat Fiore said I should start scheduling workouts on my calendar, as I would any other appointment. This makes sense to me, because there have been days when I lay out my sweats and sneakers with the best of intentions but simply forget to put them on. (Yes, I have bought ginkgo, but—no joke—I keep forgetting to take it.) I took Pat's suggestion and entered a workout into my PalmPilot. It was a session at InForm Fitness, the city's gym of the moment, which specializes in Super Slow weight training and promises that you need exercise for only thirty minutes a week to get in shape. Even I have thirty minutes a week. I kept the appointment and am proud to report that although my body was exactly the same shape, parts of it really hurt.

What I needed was incentive. My friend Bonnie Rothman Morris, a journalist and screenwriter, motivates herself to fit exercise around work by turning exercise *into* work. She took a job as a spin instructor at our local health club. Not only is there money to spur her on, there is also the fact that she burns enough calories to eat all the ice cream she wants. (Wouldn't work for me—I'm not that crazy about ice cream and I detest spinning.)

Mike Augustyniak, a former fullback for the New York Jets and now a desk-bound insurance salesman in Melbourne, Florida, propelled himself to the gym every morning on the force of a bet. He and four equally competitive friends wagered two hundred dollars each that they could lose 10 percent of their body weight within six months. Those who made weight would split the kitty and spend it on a golf weekend.

I don't play golf. And in order to place a bet with my friends, I would have to tell them what I weigh, so that is out of the question. But there are all different forms of peer pressure. I scheduled my next thirty-minute workout, then wrote about that fact in a column. I wagered that such a very public announcement—and the resulting humiliation if I canceled—would inspire me to show up.

RILEY, THE DOG

It is time that I officially introduce all of you to the newest member of my family. Riley Belkin Gelb is the Wheaten terrier puppy who has been doing his best to keep me from writing this (or anything else, for that matter) by licking my fingers whenever I start to type.

A lot of attention has been given to the challenges of balancing work and children. Yet what about the challenge of balancing work and pets? When I first began writing from home, I felt guilt every time I shooed my children out of the office. But I stood firm, determined to draw the line between home and work. Now it is Riley who wants attention during work hours, and I find I have no backbone at all. Evan's room was painted recently so he had to spend one night sleeping on the pullout sofa next to my desk. The dog came in the next morning and decided he really liked the new arrangement. We now call it Riley's bed and he sits on it all day, like a pampered pasha, taking up both physical and psychic space. (Sorry, Sande.)

I'm told that there are dogs who help their humans work.

Jeff Steen, a management consultant in San Francisco, uses his Jake, a sixteen-month-old mix of Labrador retriever and Rhodesian Ridgeback, in place of a clock. The duo is at their desk (one in front of it, the other under it) by 8 A.M. At 4 P.M., Jeff said, Jake's "job is to make me take a break" so that Jake can take a walk. At about 7 P.M. "he makes certain that I know it is time for play by placing his toy ever so gently in my crotch. That is kind of like the old whistle in the factory that signals the end of the shift."

Not Riley. Although quite organized (he places all his chew toys within reach on his oversized bed) and efficient (he can find a banana peel within moments of knocking over the trash) and well versed in the ways of modern communication (he jumps up and heads for the door every time AOL says "Good-bye"), he would not qualify as anyone's idea of an executive assistant. In the time it took me to write these paragraphs, he whimpered to be let out three times. When we came back in from the last (unproductive) walk, he stole a pen off my desk and ate it.

I realize things could be worse. Sarah Imrie, a literary publicist in Manhattan, shares her home office with Abby, a five-year-old Lab mix, and Jaspar, a four-year-old cat of questionable lineage. Jaspar "has a pathological obsession with the fax-copier machine," Sarah said, and so he attacks and then shreds any document as it is faxed, "the more important, the better." Abby, in turn, "has a deep-seated hatred of all uniformed delivery personnel," leading her to bark uncontrollably throughout the day, usually "when I am on the phone with clients."

Sarah and I would not have these pet problems, of course,

if we worked in an office. We would have different pet problems. According to a study by the American Animal Hospital Association, 75 percent of pet owners feel guilty about leaving their animals at home while they go to work, and 38 percent admit to calling home to talk to those animals. To relieve our guilt and their bladders, we hire dog walkers and pet-sitters, then race home in the middle of the day when the people we hire don't show up.

There is a mini-trend afoot allowing employees to bring their pets to the office, which has led to some interesting company memos. At Netscape in San Francisco all new employees were given a copy of the "Policy on Dogs in the Workplace," which said, among other things: no dogs with fleas; no dogs that bark too much; no dogs in the restrooms or cafeterias or business meetings; dogs may not snatch food off other people's desks; all receptionists will keep a supply of doggy cleanup bags. NewsEdge, in Burlington, Massachusetts, had a similar set of rules, including a "three accidents and you're out" dictum for dogs who are not house-trained (remind me never to bring Riley to News-Edge). The company provided vacuums to owners of dogs who shed.

To every trend there is a naysayer, and Howard Mellin, of the Good Dog training school in downtown Chicago, warned that spending all day with your dog might cause neuroses (he was speaking of the pet, not the owner). Of the nearly five hundred dogs he trains each year, Mellin said, almost half suffer from separation anxiety and low self-esteem. The reason, he thinks, is that so many people are working at home or bringing their dogs to the office that the animals forget how to cope when the owner is not around.

Okay, Riley, I am going out to lunch now, just so you don't get too used to me. While I'm gone, maybe you can learn to growl at the telemarketers?

GIVING

IN TO WORK

THE INTERNET
BABY'S BIRTHDAY

Ry Sidney Cohen is nearly two years old. When he was born in the summer of 2000 to Aaron Cohen and Nina del Rio, he was the first baby ever born to any of the two-hundred-plus employees at Concrete Media, the Internet company founded by his dad. His pending birth caused all sorts of tumult. There was talk of maternity/paternity leave, of on-site day care, and of parents who might actually want to get home for dinner.

Let me remind you what Aaron said shortly before his son arrived. "I'll take a week off immediately after the baby is born," he vowed, "and a total of six weeks in the first six months. My intention is to be a highly focused father. I understand that it's important to balance my life. I'm determined to figure out how to do it.

"We see this company as being around for a long, long time," he continued back then. "We need to hit a stride that is sustainable over the long haul. If I can't learn how to be a parent and an executive, then I can't imagine how I can ask my employees to do that."

Here's what Aaron thinks of that plan today: "Everything I said in that article didn't happen," he says now that he is actually a parent. "Not one thing."

The first thing that didn't happen was Aaron's time off. His baby was born at the exact moment that the Internet economy started to fail and the company he had built began to fall apart. "The market completely disappeared for the services," he says. "We built Internet businesses. Our clients— the Avons, the Tommy Hilfigers—they stopped investing simultaneously. Of the fifteen publicly traded companies who did what we did, five are already out of business, and five more are well on their way."

Expecting to work less after Ry was born, Aaron had staffed Concrete Media with talented people who could run day-to-day operations while he learned to be a father. But though these people "were more than equipped to run the company," he says, "they weren't equipped to handle its unraveling."

That was Aaron's job. So he went right back in and did it. He worked "seven days a week" to save his creation, changing its name, changing its focus, whittling the business until there was nothing left to save. His time with Ry became condensed into the hours between six and eight-thirty each morning, but even then there were distractions. "Hiring two hundred people then firing two hundred people is brutal," he says, his voice still heavy with sadness. "I spent the first eight months of his life trying to save my company and my people's jobs."

Ry was born in July. Concrete Media closed completely the following April. Aaron took the next three months off, to clear his head and get to know his son. "Who could have known how extraordinary it is to have a kid?" he says. "Those months off with him are the silver lining. There is no question that our family life is richer than it was a year ago."

Finally ready to go back to the working world, Aaron began planning a new business, one which helps other entrepreneurs get started. "Our goal is to bring talented entrepreneurs to the point of critical mass where they can attract their first round of capital," he explains, putting his CEO voice back on. "We raised one hundred million dollars for Concrete Media. We know how to raise money."

Aaron's business partner also has a young child, and much of the motivation behind their new plan "has to do with having time for our families. We dictate when we see our kids. That's a very big deal."

So while they are hoping to help others grow huge companies, they also plan to keep theirs small. "Right now, it's just the two of us with two clients," he says. "That's a good start. I think I'll be cautious about hiring a lot more people in the future because of what I've been through."

The unpredictable mysteries of business have made him more prepared to be a parent, he says. Or maybe it's the other way around. Whichever came first, and wherever it all leads, he is trying to enjoy the ride.

"When I last talked to you I was the chief executive of a fast-growing company and a guy who didn't really get what it meant to be a father," he says. "Now everything is inchoate. It's a tremendous sense of discovery. It's a wonderful, scary moment."

VACATION

The big vacation question when I was a kid was whether we would fly or drive. The big vacation question now that I am a grown-up is whether to take the laptop or go cold turkey.

Bruce and I have a tradition of working while playing. It began on our Hawaiian honeymoon, when my new husband spent the plane ride reading medical journals and I was awakened at an ungodly hour by *The New York Times Magazine* so I could answer questions from a fact checker. Then there was the memorable summer on Block Island when I had to finish the final draft of a book and Bruce had a grant application due. We were sharing a rental house with my sister-in-law and brother-in-law, and between the four of us, we'd brought four cell phones, three laptops, and a fax machine.

This does, I admit, seem to go against the basic meaning of the word *vacation,* and I've learned that there are other couples who handle things differently. Cathy Seibel, for instance, is a federal prosecutor who refuses to even think about work while on vacation. Her staff knows that "I only want to be called if Martians have landed in my office," and, thankfully, that hasn't happened yet. Cathy's husband, on the other hand, is a self-diagnosed work addict. A physician and medical historian at New York–Presbyterian Hospital, Dr. Barron Lerner feels that time spent away from work is time spent worrying about work piling up—in other words, only by working can he relax.

In the days before laptops, Cathy and Barron would venture to the Vineyard for just a week at a time because she got agitated if he worked, and he got agitated if he didn't. Then, with the coming of the E-mail era, they agreed to be daring and try a two-week vacation. But first they established some carefully crafted ground rules. He was allowed to work. But only during one of the two weeks. And only at night after their two children were asleep. "You have to do what fits each person's desires and neuroses," he said.

Theirs is an evolving compromise. There is some question, for instance, about whether E-mails fall under the no-work-during-daylight clause. "I regard that as work, absolutely, but he regards it as an activity of daily living," said Cathy. And there are varying interpretations of what counts as vacation literature, too. Barron would argue that the 581-page biography of legendary physician William Osler "could qualify as a beach book."

Gail Wiggin, founder of Aabalone Red, a Web development company, also sees vacation as a badly timed interruption of work. In the old days, she said, she would spin herself into a frenzy in the hours before V-Day, trying to tie up all the loose ends at work and at home. Now she takes what she calls "the dot.com.mom vacation," which means scheduling her family's departure twenty-four hours ahead of her own, then spending that full day "at warp speed," working virtually nonstop. "I don't have to cook, eat, answer the telephone, or be sociable," she said.

Knowing that "every tiny bit of work is done" means she can put that work aside for a while. On the inaugural test of her approach, a family reunion in New Hampshire, she "even decided not to even plug in the brand-new rocket ship Powerbook from which I had hitherto been inseparable." The dot.com.mom approach is only effective, she cautioned, if you apply it on the other end, too—leaving vacation a day before everyone else and spending twenty-four hours excavating your desk.

I can't see that either of these solutions will work for us. The dot.com.mom vacation, for instance, requires a marriage where only one spouse has an over-enmeshed relationship with their work. At our house we would spend so much time jockeying to be the one who stayed home that I don't think we'd ever actually leave on our trip. Because the disturbing fact is, neither of us really minds bringing some work along. The laptop doesn't mar our vacation so much as it permits us to take one. If I could not have finished my book on Block Island, I couldn't have gone to Block Island. How lovely then that technology allows me to work in a hammock.

RANDOM THOUGHTS FROM THE MIDDLE OF THE NIGHT

At the moment, I have jet lag. I want to sleep when I should be awake, I'm wide awake when I should be asleep, and I crave breakfast at the most unreasonable hours. It is an unexpectedly familiar feeling—not because I'm some international jet-setter, but because I suffer from a form of jet lag even when I haven't gone anywhere. We each have an internal body clock. Mine has long been out of sync with the clock that rules my life and my work.

If my personal clock had its way, it would wake me up at about ten in the morning and we would amble into the office. We would start our day slowly—opening the mail, answering phone calls—then we would have lunch. At two o'clock we would snap into efficient and energetic gear, writing furiously, barely looking up until seven o'clock or (much) later. I realized with delight and relief years ago that my natural rhythm perfectly matches the rhythm of a newsroom, which is one of the many reasons I began to do what I do.

Then I had children. No more sleeping until nine or ten.

Next, I left daily journalism for a kind of writing that does not require daily deadline sprints. I still rev up mentally at two in the afternoon, anyway, but school lets out for the boys at three. Early each day I vow to become a morning person. It hasn't happened yet.

Added to this is my insomnia problem. Periodically I find myself bolt upright in bed at 2 A.M., wide awake in a way that makes it clear my sleep is over for the night. Before I knew better, I would try to drift off. Now I give in, get up, and work until dawn. While it wouldn't be my choice of a schedule, there is something cozy about sitting at the computer in the dark, sipping a cup of tea or a mug of hot chocolate. The most interesting part is that I'm not the only one awake. I have answered E-mails at the oddest hours and, minutes after I hit SEND, I've received a reply.

I looked for help in the office of Dr. Thomas M. Kilkenny, director of the Sleep Center at the Staten Island University Hospital, who said this is nothing so exotic as a rebellious body clock. It's called "sleep maintenance insomnia" and it is always a symptom of something off-kilter in the (non)sleeper's life. While the cause can be physical, he said, it is more commonly the result of what he describes as "poor sleep hygiene," or not taking the time to properly wind down at the end of the day. "A lot of go-getters are very busy until the moment they go to bed," he said. "You can't go from fourth gear on the highway to a complete stop just like that."

Instead he suggested that I shut off all "brain stimuli" (that includes the laptop and the TV) about an hour or more before bedtime. When that doesn't work, and I wake in the middle of the night anyway, he said I should relax in bed for no more than twenty minutes, and if sleep doesn't come I should leave the bedroom rather than toss and turn. After that he prescribed a softly lit room, quiet music, and a glass of milk. No computer, because that sends a wake-up signal to the brain. No caffeine (meaning no hot cocoa and no tea) because that wakes up the rest of me. I can be in control of this problem, he promised. It doesn't have to control me.

But is it always bad for the body to be in control? Ben Mezrich, for one, has turned his backward biorhythms into a lifestyle. He realized back in college that he functioned poorly during the day, so upon graduation seven years ago, he became a fiction writer "because they can set their own hours." Under the pen name Holden Scott he's had a good deal of success while working between 11 P.M. and 5 A.M. every night. He's even turned down a few "real jobs" writing for a television series because he would have to get up in the morning. "I do my best work at night," he said. "To change my schedule would mean I couldn't do my best work."

I'm far from ready to live on what Ben/Holden calls "vampire time," but I can't help noticing that I get a lot of work done in those silent, sleepless hours. So does Randall Enos, the graphic artist who for years has drawn the delightful sketches that accompany my *Times* columns. Randy regularly works all night, sometimes because work deadlines require it, but usually because that's when the creative energy starts to flow.

The key, he says, is to be prepared to "crash" midway through the next afternoon. When that happens, he gives in and takes a nap. I'd happily do that, too, Randy, but that's just about the time my children are getting home.

WHEN THE MUSE
GOES ON STRIKE

Most of this book was written in bed. Usually I was propped on top of the blankets while I wrote, but sometimes I climbed full under the covers with my laptop. It's a Pavlovian thing. When it's time to write, I plump up the pillows, turn on the laptop, lay myself down, and feel my brain start to fire. There is a desktop—with a larger screen and a more comfortable keyboard—a few steps away, but it doesn't have the same effect on my neurons.

Long ago I gave up trying to control the work and I tried letting it control me. There are times when I can write, times when I can't write, and little I can do to understand why. I've decided just to be grateful that there are ways to jump-start the muse at all.

These are among the truths I've learned since I stopped looking:

1. "Gel time" counts. Going to the supermarket, calling friends, taking a nap—all this may seem to be procrastination, but it's actually part of the creative process. While I'm

watching *West Wing,* there is a sector of my brain whirring a project round and round. The butterfly doesn't develop in the open. There's a lot of action inside that chrysalis, but from the outside it looks like a lump doing nothing at all.

2. The less personal the writing, the better it works at my desk on my PC. My magazine pieces are written there, as were my first two books. This is mostly because there are more notes involved, and notes tend to fall off the bed. But it's also because the desktop feels serious and substantial, while the laptop feels intimate and cozy. They must trigger different parts of my brain.

3. Editing should be done on the road. There are a half-dozen coffeehouses and bookshops in the neighborhood that have gotten used to my hanging around. They should be too noisy for any real work, but, to the contrary, I find my home office too quiet. Sitting amid the din at Starbucks forces me to conjure a cone of concentration so I see nothing but the words on the page.

4. When the words won't come, take a shower. If I didn't already work at home, I would have to start working at home now that I've learned how inspiring water can be. My best ledes have sprung into my head when it was covered with shampoo. Often, when I'm stuck for a way in to an idea, I go up and take a shower—not something you can do at your average workplace.

5. When that fails, go to the movies. It doesn't really matter what I watch, just that the theater is dark and cool and that it's the middle of the afternoon and I'm not supposed to be there at all. When I emerge two hours later, blinking in the afternoon sun, I usually go home with clearer vision and renewed energy.

6. When that fails, panic. That's the power of deadline. When the time comes that I *have* to work, then I do the work. It may simply be that my brain likes a good game of chicken and refuses to produce unless it counts. My husband often wonders how I can miss deadlines and stay in journalism. "I never miss the *real* deadline," I tell him, and so far I never have.

MINI-VACATIONS

Every hour or two—more often, I admit, when the writing is not going particularly well—I pause and take a small vacation. My current favorite destination is Minesweeper, the computer game. After a few minutes I return to the real world, refreshed and ready to work, at least for a little while.

These mini-vacations are absolutely not a replacement for the real thing. But they are as necessary a part of getting through the day as a real vacation is to getting through the year. Some of us admit this, some hide it. Some recognize it as a sanity break, the rest of us feel guilty that we are wasting time. What follows is a collection, culled from reader E-mails, of where and how we escape. Take five minutes now and read them. Consider it a vacation.

Doug Renfro, president of Renfro Foods, a family-owned salsa manufacturing business in Fort Worth: "I sometimes go to expedia.com or travelocity.com and plan an imaginary/fantasy trip, such as to Switzerland. It takes maybe five minutes, is interesting, and it relieves stress."

Dean William G. Christie, Owen Graduate School of

Management at Vanderbilt University: "If I have five minutes to spare between meetings and need to clear my head, I fire up Microsoft Flight Simulator. I'll typically fly a 737 or a 777, and it's a challenge, since all I have at my disposal is a mouse! It wouldn't look proper for the dean of a leading business school to have foot pedals and a force-feedback joystick in his office! I have a number of saved situations, typically landings, that I can use to test my skills. A five-minute vacation will usually involve final approach into a major airport with a self-imposed malfunction, such as loss of an engine. Nothing focuses the mind more than trying to land a 777 on one engine on short notice! I always walk away feeling refreshed, and my bags never get lost!"

Mark Porter, CEO and president of httprint in San Francisco: "I call up my little girl and practice the alphabet with her. Hannah is twenty-one months old and loves to talk on the phone. Hearing her say Daddy brings me back to earth if things are getting too crazy. I also go on to the *Boston Globe* Web site and read about how my Red Sox are doing."

Sharon Keys Seal, professional business coach in Baltimore: "My breaks are very intentional and planned; otherwise, my day just seems to sift through my fingers. One of my favorite breaks is going out for a massage at the women's center of a local hospital. Other great breaks are walking around the block (I just started wearing a pedometer so that I can make sure I walk at least 10,000 steps per day) and a midday call to my best friend in Missouri, on her day off. A quick call to my parents in Texas, which they love. And, on a really hot day, a midday shower to cool off and wake up."

Peg Church, elementary school counselor in Philadelphia: "I juggle meetings with mini-crises, recognizing that my time is never my own. For relief, I turn to a wonderful, all-natural citrus spray. A few spritzes around the room and I feel myself uplifted and energized."

Robert Volmer, of Crosby-Volmer Communications in Washington: "There is nothing better to relieve the stress of work than to watch a bunch of kids play baseball. Almost every hit ends up being a home run, even though the ball rarely passes the pitcher's mound. The pitcher will over-throw the ball to first base, and the batter keeps running to second. This process usually repeats itself until the player has safely reached home plate. Seeing the light in their eyes and the fun they are having lets the everyday hassles of the office dissipate, if only for an hour."

Angela Henry, a partner in the executive search firm of Ray & Berndtson: "I visit old lobbies," to marvel at the archi-tecture. "It's like going to a museum but without the usual restrictions: I can slurp my Frappuccino, it's free, nobody tells me to move along, and I don't have to listen to pseudo art critics pretending they know all about the artist's intent."

Tom Dilatush, CEO of Previo, a San Diego technology company: "I save up particularly pleasant little tasks (telling someone about a promotion, handing out a little positive feedback, etc.) for when I need a break. Then I make a point of leaving my office to go do that task. The combination gets my mind off whatever I was concentrating on, or it lets me concentrate on something pleasant as a break from the chaos. It gives me a nice break either way."

WORKING AFTER WORK

Have you ever met an ophthalmologist at a bar and asked if you're a candidate for laser surgery? If not, then you've never been out drinking with Dr. Sandra C. Belmont. "As soon as I tell anyone what I do, that's all they want to talk about," said Sandra, the director of the New York Weill Cornell Medical Center Laser Vision Correction Center.

Have you ever cornered a real estate broker at a cocktail party and started describing your home? "They all want to know how much their apartments are worth," said Marilyn Harra Kaye, president of her own real estate brokerage in Manhattan. At a recent conference in California about Buddhism, she said, amid the meditating and the tai chi, a stranger came over to chat about her place on East Ninetieth Street.

In this 24/7, market-manic world, there is a lot of talk about workaholics who won't let go of their work. Yet what about people who would—if only the rest of us would let them? "I have no fun at parties," said Bonnie Russell, an Internet strategist in Southern California and one of my most prolific E-mail pals, "because complete strangers think nothing of asking me how I do what I do. I realize that the Internet is sexy. But if I'm standing around in a sexy outfit, I certainly don't want to be appreciated for my brains."

Dr. Marty Becker has resigned himself to the fact that he can't work on an airplane. He is a veterinarian (and a regular guest on *Good Morning America*) and on a flight from New York to Boston once his seatmate spent the hour telling stories about Holly, the collie. "I've been in the dentist chair having root canal and the dentist started asking about how to litter box–train his cat," he said. And this is not, he insists, because he's on television. It's because he's a vet. "A friend of mine was at death's door, with tubes going everywhere, fearing he might not make it. A cute redheaded nurse comes in and says, 'You probably don't remember me, but I brought my cat to you. Now I'm having a problem with hairballs . . .' "

Amy Potozkin tried to avoid the talk-about-work trap on first dates by signing up with a dating service. As a casting director with the Berkeley Repertory Theater, actors have approached her at funerals looking for work, so she told the agency that she did not want to meet any actors. Her first match was a businessman. What he didn't mention on his application was that he acted in local community theater. "We spent the rest of the date talking about whether or not he should quit his job and take his acting career to the next level," Amy recalled with a grimace.

The after-work requests for stock tips became so intrusive for Cody Acree, a securities analyst in Dallas, that he began to lie. "My wife and I went to a B&B to get away from the stress, but when I sat down at breakfast I was inundated with questions from the other guests," he explained. "So now I tell people I'm a janitor, and they don't seem to want to talk."

Cody is not the only one who lies. Marty Becker has told strangers he is an "award-winning insurance salesman." Amy Potozkin has said she is a waitress. Bonnie Russell has introduced herself at parties as a librarian, unless the man doing the asking was particularly attractive—in which case she has said she is a masseuse.

GETTING BACK

TO WORK

SEASONAL GUILT

When I was first promoted from phone-ignoring clerk to inexperienced-but-eager reporter I was given the consumer affairs beat. My family found this very funny, since I had spent a lifetime losing receipts and failing to fill out warranty cards.

Early in my tenure I wrote a long, detailed article about how to choose an air-conditioner, riffing about energy efficiency ratings and BTUs per square cubic foot of space. A week after that article ran, my own ancient window unit broke. What did the wise consumer reporter do? She picked up the phone and begged for help from her dad.

I'm good at giving advice. I'm not quite as good at taking it. This fact became spectacularly clear after I had been writing the Life's Work column for about a year. I'd practiced a lot of what I preached during those twelve months. I was good at carving time out from work to enjoy my life, and I was good at shutting out my life when a deadline loomed. It was the times in between that I wasn't very good at. The normal days, when there wasn't a pressing event like a school play or a sick child—just a cute kid who wanted to kick a soccer ball around before it got dark. The average days, when I wasn't racing to finish, but simply laying groundwork for a future project.

On those days—meaning most days—I was in a self-created, inefficient, unsettling kind of limbo. I could work whenever I wanted. I could take a break from work any time, too. So how the heck was I supposed to decide? And why, no matter what I chose to do, did I feel guilty about what I had chosen not to do?

After one particularly lazy, and therefore guilt-ridden, summer, I vowed to buckle back down and have a system. I made new rules for myself—certain hours at the computer, certain hours at the gym. I made lots of new rules for the children—mostly about when they could and could not enter the office or use my computer. I tried making rules for the dog. All this worked—for a little while. But by the following summer my discipline had slipped completely, and come autumn I started over again.

It was sometime in September that I had my revelation in the pediatrician's office. I was trying to do the impossible, control the uncontrollable. I didn't abandon my yearly scramble to regroup and take charge, but I came to recognize it for what it was—the first stitches of a quilt, one that will keep me warm for a while but will inevitably unravel. As I start, then slip, then start and slip again, I'm beginning to see that this is not failure; it's an ongoing ritual. I'm newly organized and energized in the fall, productive from winter into spring, scattered and hopeless in the summer, and on and on and on.

So now I feel guilty only about half of the time.

SEPTEMBER 2000

Once every year I feel an itch to stock up on pens and note-books and index cards. It's a lot like shopping for back-to-school supplies, except that these are back-to-*work* supplies. My apologies to Julius Caesar and Dick Clark, but the real year—the work year—begins in September.

Years of conditioning—from grade school through grad school—have led us to expect that the summer should feel different, and because we expect it, it is so. We arrive at work later, leave earlier, take long weekends. Even rush hour comes at different times. Those responsible for our mental health set the pace and lead the way. Late one August I started work on a magazine article that required interviewing a lot of psychiatrists, and although I placed calls to two dozen of them, I did not reach a single one until after Labor Day.

Not surprisingly, businesses rearrange themselves around this ebb in the calendar. The owners of We Take the Cake, a mail-order bakery based in Fort Lauderdale, analyzed their orders and saw a dramatic dip over the summer. "People are traveling, businesses don't have events going on," said Kathy

Guerke, who owns the company with her husband, Andy. And then there's the added problem of customers who diet to fit into their swimsuits. So the Guerkes close shop completely for two weeks in July, taking a busman's holiday to the south of France, where they eat a lot of desserts. On their return, they cut back their hours, closing every day at 2 P.M. "The summer schedule will probably last until November," said Kathy, who was just back from playing tennis at three o'clock one August Monday afternoon.

Susan Buckley is a senior vice president and partner of a marketing services agency based in Cincinnati. Her company is too busy to shut down completely, she said, but does other things to "make it up to our employees," who would really rather be outside. Every Wednesday from June through August there is a catered lunch out on the patio. Each Thursday a truck with a water tank comes to the parking lot and washes employees' cars, courtesy of the company. Fridays are half days, Susan said, because very little work gets done on Friday afternoons. "Why bother making calls," she asked, "when all you do is reach people's phone mail?"

There are, of course, workers who beg to differ. "I work harder in August than I do in September, that's for sure," said Len Ferber, a Chicago lawyer. He certainly sounded tired. "If a client is going on vacation," he said, "he's either going to give you a lot of work to finish by the time he leaves, so he can tell his boss, 'I got this done, I got that done.' Or else he's going to give you a lot of work to finish while he's on vacation so it's ready when he gets back." In a roundabout way, I'd argue, this proves my very point. Mr. Ferber works so hard in the summer because his clients do not.

Several years ago I was writing a book proposal over the

summer, and my agent was urging me to work quickly so that she could send it to publishers during September. (I should note that these pep talks to write faster never came on Friday afternoons, because she closed her office on Fridays during the summer.) September, she warned, was the only time anyone got any real work done in publishing. Come October, it seems, everyone is distracted by the Frankfurt book fair. In November there's Thanksgiving followed by a month of parties, meaning no one can concentrate until the new year. The doldrums of January and February are, well, doldrums, interrupted by another booksellers' convention, this one in London, in March. Then there's spring break— planning for it, then recovering from it—and before you can click on your PalmPilot, it's Memorial Day.

Which brings us to Labor Day, aptly named because it marks the start of the only few productive weeks of the year. Now sharpen those #2 pencils. You're going back to work.

MY NEW COMPUTER

After years of writing at home, I broke down and bought a brand-new computer. Yes, it was faster than the five-year-old model that it replaced; and no, it didn't grind aloud while it thought; and true, it was attached to a brand-new printer, which added color to my writing and printed black and white at twice the rate of its predecessor (may it rest in peace). But none of this was the best part. The addition of this computer meant our house now had two—and that meant I finally got my office back.

In households everywhere, there is a generational turf war over the computer. Whether you work at home or bring work home, I'll wager you've had to arm wrestle for keyboard time if you share disk space with anyone over the age of five. Ron Katz and his wife, Rita Rigano, thought they had worked this problem out when they founded Penguin Human Resource Consulting in the basement of their New Rochelle, New York, home. They had three computers when they began—two moderately new Pentiums for Mom and Dad and a nine-year-old 486 SX25 for their three children. But the kids turned up their noses at the dinosaur, which couldn't connect to the Internet or run their games. Instead, they trooped into the office to use one of the new computers, often with their friends in tow.

"They'd work on a school project and leave their pages," Ron said. "It's bad enough having to find things in my mess, but I also have to wade through their mess." Added Rita: "I can't have the whole neighborhood in here looking at my invoices."

So Penguin Human Resource Consulting upgraded and networked. They hauled Ron's old computer across the hall, into the half of the basement that is the rec room, and positioned it "in such a way that when you walk in the door you will be able to see what's on the screen," he said, to protect their children from the evils of the Internet. Then Ron got a new machine, one that is password protected, which kept his children from accessing it for at least a little while.

At our house we resisted buying the second computer for a very long time. Part of the reason was the cost. Even though prices have dropped dramatically compared to what they were, they are still very high compared to what I casually spend. But there was something else at work here, too, something more primal and psychological than simple economics. Just as it probably was in the earliest years of the automobile and the telephone, owning one of these machines feels practical, while owning more than one seems self-indulgent.

I simply can't decide whether to treat this piece of technology like a telephone, a television, or a typewriter. I was imprinted from childhood with very different sets of rules for each one. A typewriter, for instance, was something every child should have, and I still own the one I was given the year I turned nine. A television set, on the other hand, was something no child should have, and a telephone was a "maybe," but only after age sixteen and never a private line. My parents didn't care that "everyone else" had a TV in their room and their own phone number. I always suspected that the very fact that everyone else was doing it was one of the reasons we were not.

Several decades later not "everyone" owns a second computer, but a surprising number—25 percent of American households—do. Perhaps because my children are wiser or craftier than I was, they never directly lobbied to join those ranks. Instead they elbowed. "Mom, this is due tomorrow," Evan would fret, as he paced by my desk waiting to type up a school project. "Are you finished working yet?"

So we moved my old machine down to the family room, where, as in the Katzes' house, you can see the screen as soon as you walk in the door. A state-of-the-art replacement purrs on my desktop, which has been cleared of piles of drafts about the Algonquin and the Iroquois and nearly all the stacks of computer games. It's quieter in my office, but the boys still stop in to "visit" now and then. That's because it took them less than an hour to realize that their machine has only a dial-up modem and mine has DSL.

ORGANIZE (AGAIN)

Everyone has a task they put off until it becomes infinitely more dreadful. Mine is filing my expenses. An equally delinquent friend insists there is deep pathology at work here, and that our real fear, rooted in childhood, is that a "father figure" will reprimand us for having spent too much. All I know is that I "lend" various publications frightening amounts of money because I can't get my expense statements out on time.

For most of my working life I had a system. I would routinely shove all my receipts into my wallet. When there was no room for even one more, I would give in and fill out my expense account, a method that kept me only two or three months behind. About a year ago, however, I began receiving memos from the publications for whom I write insisting that expenses were due no more than sixty days after the money was spent. For some reason this paralyzed me. I began taking the stacks of receipts out of my wallet with every intention of filing them but would become sidetracked along the way. The piles of eensy papers would sit on my desk, falling first onto the floor and then into oblivion.

I needed help. That's when I hired Sande Nelson. She came to my home office, cleared herself that space on my cluttered couch, and asked me a lot of questions. Then, on a sweltering Saturday morning in September she came back with an eighteen-page plan of attack, prepared to spend as long as it might take (at the rate of $70 an hour) to get me organized.

There are two kinds of organizers, and Sande is more therapist than drill sergeant, more artist than automaton, which is probably a good thing for a client who arguably lives in fear of authority. She also turns out to be somewhat disorganized herself and hasn't yet figured out how to use a computer or check the voice mail on her new, first-ever cell phone. This worried me, I admit, but it also made her less intimidating. Her sympathetic phrase of choice is "I hear you," which she repeated regularly throughout the afternoon, even when I wasn't saying anything. For the record, she agreed that I have a deep-rooted problem but diagnosed it as completion anxiety—a fear that I will finish and realize I am not perfect, which is why I never finish. My father will be pleased to learn that I am not afraid of him, after all.

Our day of organizing began with a supply list. Shopping. I knew I could complete *that*. Sande had everything listed by store and reference number. Among her suggestions: a $1,200 set of cherry filing cabinets and a new photocopying machine. I didn't buy those. But I did load up on hundreds of file folders, dozens of file jackets, and thousands of colored self-adhesive file labels, which are the key to this whole exercise.

When my office was all but filled with bags from Office Depot and Staples, we set out to overhaul my filing system. With Sande at my side, I passed judgment on every file that I have, deciding what to keep and where to keep it. I filled a mound of trash bags with historical documents including the lease on an apartment I have not lived in since 1991. I slapped a COLUMN IDEAS label on a large brown file jacket, then filled it with the two dozen separate piles of paper that had been stacked haphazardly around the room. The notes for a months-old magazine article were filed in a closet Sande labeled ARCHIVES.

Most of my newly alphabetized and categorized files now sit in long cardboard storage boxes under one window. The files that are the backbone of my custom-tailored expense account system, however, are in plainer sight, on the wall next to my desk, where I cannot possibly ignore them. Per Sande's instructions, I have broken the entire awful process into tiny baby steps. Each step is a labeled folder: RECEIPTS TO BE EXPENSED, EXPENSED RECEIPTS, TO BE PHOTO-COPIED, PHOTOCOPIED EXPENSES, TO BE SENT, EXPENSES SENT, TO BE REIMBURSED, and REIMBURSED EXPENSES, 2001. The trick is to move the pieces of paper from one file to the next so I never lose track of what has yet to be done. Every Friday morning, according to Sande, I must sit down with these files and just do it.

On the morning after her visit I buckled down and completed the paperwork for articles dating back nine months. For months of subsequent Fridays I have dutifully followed her instructions and gotten statements out on time. One day I might even feel confident enough to tackle a new organizing project: clearing out my supply closet to make room for all the folders and adhesive labels that now rule my life. Sande has a looming project, too. She has bought a laptop and is learning how to print her labels.

CALENDARS

There's a small gift to working parents on the calendar every few years. When Halloween falls on a Sunday. That means no racing home for trick or treat. No sending them off with someone else because we can't make it back in time, and no starting out so late that the youngest ones, already overwhelmed by the anticipation of it all, completely fall apart.

We have five overworked calendars at our house—my husband and I each carry an electronic pocket "brain," on my desk sits a more old-fashioned leather date book, the school-issued version is in the basement, and a jumbo model swings on the back of the kitchen door. (Sande says that part of my problem is a lack of calendar consolidation.) If you put them all together, they are an argument for human cloning. Bruce bought us the PalmPilots because they can "talk" to each other. Okay, that's a start. But what I need is technology that can allow me to meet with my editor *and* the second-grade teacher at the same time.

Fact is, there are countless reasons not to be at work. The first day of school. Yearly checkups, especially ones that include *shots*. Columbus Day, when schools are closed but so many businesses are open. (Last-minute tickets to opening day—but that's a whole other category.) The afternoon I left my father's bedside in the cardiac care unit to talk about turning my book into a movie with a producer who would be in town only a few hours. (Her interest turned out to be fleeting; my father, I'm relieved to report, is now faster on the treadmill than I am.)

True, flex-time, job-sharing, four-day workweeks, and the Family Leave Act have all been created to address the problem, but what I'm talking about isn't really about rules. However many sanctioned days off we're given, there will always be one more worthy distraction, not to mention the small matter of getting the work done. So the squares of the calendar will continue to be an oversized board game, a daily accumulation of choices that together shape a life. Do I use my get-out-of-jail-free card for the class play or the class trip? I'll trade my Martin Luther King Jr.'s birthday for the baby's first birthday and a holiday to be named later.

Once in a while the answers are obvious. They jump off the calendar in sharp relief, putting everything else in perspective. At a gathering of my monthly book club, a group of us who thought our lives were busy listened in sobered silence as one of our number described her eight-year-long legal battle with the doctors whose mistakes left her young son heartbreakingly disabled. The malpractice trial was to begin the next day and would last for weeks. "I *will* be there," she said with uncluttered certainty, despite the fact that her own business would fall into chaotic limbo while she spent all those days in court. "No question. I *will* be there."

Most of the time the choices are murkier. We can do any

given thing, but we can't do everything, which is why over-the-counter ulcer medications seem to sell so well. One of the first notes I received when I started writing my column was from Sherri Steinfeld, a freelance book publicist, who wondered: "Is this what parenting in the early twenty-first century comes down to—choosing the option that makes us feel the least guilty?" Yes, Sherri, it is. The scale that balances work and life is weighted by two questions: How many events can I tuck in and still get the job done? How many can I miss and still feel complete?

So we do what we always tell our children to do—only the best that we can. To wit, our schedule the week that Halloween last fell on a Sunday. Bruce and I missed the class trip to the pumpkin patch on Monday, but we both made it to the parent-teacher conference on Tuesday. On Wednesday I squeezed in an hour at Pumpkin Pal Day, when the children were told to invite a friend (read: *parent*) to help decorate the pumpkins. And on Friday I arrived in the middle of the costume parade across the soccer field.

But on the day itself my two scary skeletons went trick-or-treating and their two parents took them. Their grandparents came over early to snap some photos, and we had time to make a party of it all. The next morning we regrouped to face the question of November. Is the Friday after Thanksgiving a holiday, or what?

Homework gets harder as children grow. Now in addition to my usual business travel arrangements—plane reservations, hotel reservations, car rental, driving directions—I find myself worrying about one thing more: Will there be access to a fax machine at about five o'clock eastern standard time, so Evan and Alex can fax me their homework?

There's a trend at our house when it comes to business travel. When Bruce does it, someone back home always gets sick. He was in Vienna when Evan was ordered to spend an immobile weekend on the couch because of an inflammation of his hip joint and in San Jose when the poor boy spent another weekend on the same couch because of a broken leg. So there was a lot of consulting and consoling done long-distance.

When I travel, the glitches (knock wood) have been more mundane. I've scheduled play dates from a street corner in Denver and hired a roofer from a hotel room in Louisville. One night when my plane was very late and Alex was very young, I sang him a lullaby from the Atlanta airport. It was the Barney song, and it made the women at the phones on either side of me start to cry. It might have been my voice, but I prefer to think it was the universal tug of a fretful child who is far away.

Leaving the house doesn't mean you leave the house behind. And now that the boys are older, their needs go beyond simple lullabies, which is why we've hit upon the homework plan. They fax their worksheets to me, I fax my suggestions back, they send revisions, and I fax or phone with my praise. And somehow I also manage to fit in the meetings I came for in the first place. (Let me preempt your letters here. Yes, Bruce could check the work when he gets home, but by that late hour my sons are so tired that the exercise would be torture for everyone.)

If I dared to suggest again that all this technology is a mixed blessing—we *can* be in touch; ergo, we feel we *must*—my mother would probably remind me of the night she was born. She arrived a month ahead of schedule and my grandfather was three thousand miles away on a business trip. My grandmother sent him a telegram, which he didn't get until the next morning. He boarded a train and nearly a week later he was home.

I say my mother *probably* would remind me of this story, because I can't ask her right now. She's in South America. Her work keeps her out of the country as often as she is in it, and she revels in the technology that allows her to run her home without actually being there. She has called from an airplane to wish me a happy birthday, and from the balcony of her cruise ship to test her new cell phone. Once she called from the southernmost tip of Chile, asking me to throw out the expired milk in her fridge.

My children joke that Grandma and Grandpa should just give up the house and live out of a suitcase, but even that doesn't free you from the long-distance details. Bello Nock, the star clown of the Big Apple Circus, lives out of a custom-designed double-wide trailer, and his biggest stress, he says, is paying the bills. Or, more precisely, *finding* the bills, which is no simple task when you play eleven cities each year. His credit card statements are mailed to his "home" address in Florida, then forwarded to the circus's main office in New York, which sends them overnight to wherever he happens to be. By the time they arrive, they are often overdue, but when he calls and explains that he is a circus clown he is usually forgiven.

Forgiveness, however, is not always so easily won. Scott Kelly, the pilot on the space shuttle crew that repaired the Hubble telescope, learned this when telling his young daughter that Daddy would be in outer space on Christmas Day. To ease the blow, Lieutenant Commander Kelly promised he would aim the $2 billion piece of equipment at the North Pole just for her and peer in on Santa Claus.

He didn't do it, of course, but it's the thought that counts—the need to be home even when (especially when) you can't. Will it be a giant leap forward or backward for mankind, I wonder, when astronauts start checking math homework, singing lullabies, and paying their VISA bills while (far) away at work?

SATURDAY NIGHT

Time, according to commercials from at least one credit card company, is priceless. What costs is the stuff we fill it with. Airlines, on the other hand, can tell us the exact price of our time. Or, more specifically, the price of a Saturday night.

Not long ago, my work required a five-night trip to Seattle—arrive late Monday and take the red-eye home on Friday so I could spend Saturday with Bruce and the boys. The friendly ticket agent explained that since I'd called (twelve hours) too late to qualify for a seven-day advance purchase, the fare would be $1,898. I, in turn, explained that I wanted to buy a *seat,* not the entire *plane.* Sounding a touch less friendly, she clicked her keyboard for a while, then asked if I might consider staying over until Sunday morning. That fare would be $366.

Thankfully, this was not my money I was spending; it was my employer's. And while I do not waste anyone's money easily, at least I had the option of booking the high-priced ticket. But because big businesses are *able* to pay, small businesses are in turn *forced* to pay, and the smallest-business people have no choice but to give up their Saturday nights. One friend, who is completing a book, schedules all his out-of-town interviews on weekends, constantly weighing the savings in airfare against the days lost with his family. The irony, he says, is that flying out on a Thursday and home on a Monday costs hundreds of dollars less than flying out on a Monday and back on a Thursday—despite the fact that he is still taking up a (cramped) seat on Thursday and Monday.

Business travel is hardly the only facet of life where time can be traded for money. But most of the other ones make sense. Pay a few dollars more to an overnight delivery service and the package actually arrives first thing the next morning. Pay $1,532 more to an airline, and you don't get there any faster, nor is there any decrease in the level of abuse.

Sensing that we're near the breaking point, airlines have started retrofitting their cabins so that "full economy" passengers can have a whopping three to seven more inches of legroom. But even in the bigger seats, lunch is still served (squashed) in a paper bag (when it is served at all), headphones still cost extra, and though you get frequent-flier miles for your loyalty and your trouble, you don't get any more than the guy next to you, whose flight you are subsidizing. And just wait until it's time to redeem them. Early one December I tried to book our summer vacation. I was told the frequent-flier allotment of seats was already sold out on every flight to Shannon, Ireland, for the last two weeks in July.

True, if you pay a full coach fare or have enough of those hard-earned miles, there are ways of finagling your way into first class. But lately those upgrades are as hard to come by as my reward tickets to Ireland.

And true, if you've earned enough miles, the rules say you may board the plane early, meaning you might find a place for your overhead luggage, but this, too, is more theory than not. "We are pleased to preboard our Elite Card holders," the steward says, and everyone in the waiting area stands up. In front of me on the "preboard" line during one flight was a man whose Oxford health insurance card was more or less the same color as the airline's membership card. He flashed it and ambled on.

You do get two things for your extra money, however. First, the fare is fully refundable. In other words, for $1,532 more they generously allow you to cancel the flight without penalty. In the case of my Seattle trip this was no small bene-fit, because the person I was supposed to interview there backed out at the last minute and I had to scramble to reschedule.

The second perk is even more important. I learned about it on a January flight to San Francisco when headwinds meant the plane had to take on extra fuel and the airline had to bump thirty passengers to allow for the added weight. All around me, people were outraged. "For seven hundred dol-lars you'd think they'd treat you better." Or "They bumped us because we're flying on a five-hundred-dollar fare." I had paid $1,600 for my ticket, and when I checked in, the counter agent did not even mention the weight restrictions. She certainly never mentioned the idea of giving up my seat.

Pay them enough money and you're actually permitted to board the plane. Now *that's* priceless.

HOTEL ROOMS

One of the most joyous notes I ever received was from a Cornell University researcher named Alaka Basu, describing her plan to gleefully scatter her belongings around a Manhattan hotel room. Officially, she was coming to town for a board meeting. But while her employer thought work was the main reason for her trip, Alaka was most looking forward to something else.

"I love hotel rooms," she said. "They are the refuge from the deadlines on my desk, the domestic demands on my time and energy, the guilt about the treadmill. People are always complaining that they travel too much," continued Alaka, whose own schedule usually included three or four international trips each year and three or four more domestic ones. "Not me. I think a certain amount of work travel is good for people."

Count me as one of the complainers. I have a long list of gripes about business travel, and most of those have to do with the actual travel part. Once I get where I'm going though, I agree with Alaka. Sitting alone in a standard-issue hotel room, complete with room darkeners, wake-up calls, and a mini-bar, it is easy to believe you are alone in the world. In that way, business travel is different than a vacation, which usually includes family or friends and a stack of peppy guidebooks.

Alaka had not traveled for work in nearly a year, because she chose to stay home near her seventeen-year-old daughter, who was applying to college. That long gap made her crave her coming trip, and the moment she walked into her room at the Beekman Tower Hotel on Forty-ninth Street and First Avenue, she planned to fling off her shoes, drop her coat on the floor, and then "have a hot, hot shower." That done, she would order "something unhealthy" from room service and watch "something mindless" on TV. Before she leaves she would swipe the DO NOT DISTURB sign from the door and add it to her collection, which she displays on her desk instead of snapshots. "Sometimes I arrange them alphabetically," she said, "sometimes by size or color and sometimes by language."

She had a theory that "cocooning in hotel rooms is a female thing," and a very unscientific survey of my own house suggests that she's on to something. My husband hates room service. The minute he arrives at a hotel on a business trip he dumps his bags and searches for a good restaurant, ideally one that reflects the local cuisine. Me, I dump my bags and search for the room service menu and the remote control.

One night in Madison, Wisconsin, I was given a room on a concierge floor where happy-hour appetizers were offered in the evening. I was the only woman to venture into the lounge (I was wearing my Gap sweats; the men were wearing their dark suits), although the concierge assured me there were other women on the floor. "The women stay in," he said.

His explanation was that women travelers are more concerned about security and feel safer ensconced in a room. I take his point—but only to a point. True, I reflexively check the shower and closets when I enter a hotel room, although I have no idea what I would do if I actually found an intruder. I also double-bolt the door at all times, and I don't fill out the part of the room service door tag that asks "number of people in your party," because that would tip off a mad rapist that I am in the room alone.

But nerves are not the reason I order room service in the first place, and they were not Alaka's reason, either. "It's the only time I can be completely alone without guilt," she said. "Back home, if I'm not working, I need to be available to my family. I can't be selfish with my time. But because these trips are work, not a holiday, I feel free to do what I want."

HOME OFFICE CHARADES

John Lloyd, known as Jocko to those of us who are his friends and neighbors, has decided to stop pretending. He works out of his home, in a room just off the kitchen, and for seven years he was scrupulous about sounding like he was in a hushed office building. His two young sons learned to tip-toe and whisper. (So why haven't my children, who are their friends, learned this yet?) His wife, a professional musician, knew not to practice her bassoon. His clients (he works as a fund-raising consultant to nonprofits) never knew his family was there.

After spending endless energy to erase the background noise, Jocko had a most unlikely epiphany. Walking into a restaurant men's room one lunchtime, he heard someone carrying on a business call while inside a stall. If the world was ready for *that*, he reasoned, it could handle the occasional squeak or squawk from his children. So he went home and literally and metaphorically opened his office door.

"It's all about what noise is okay noise," he said. "All those people who walk down the street next to construction cranes, talking on their cell phones—that's okay? And me talking on my office phone with kids in the background—that's not okay? I reject the argument that there's a difference."

What, then, is the difference? Why has it become acceptable to announce where you're calling from—inside the airplane, stuck in traffic, the snack bar at Yankee Stadium at the top of the ninth "but I wanted to get back to you right away"—as long as the place you're calling from is not your house? My most memorable interview (aside from the one done from the couch in the Maine attorney general's office) was with an Internet mogul who spoke, with surprising clarity, from the dentist's chair. He was more than happy to tell me where he was and what type of periodontal work he was having done. My husband once sat in the waiting area of our local emergency room, stanching the bleeding from his nose with one hand and fielding phone calls from his office with the other. He felt no need to hide where he was, either.

But at home, nonoffice noise takes on a whole new meaning. The ring of the doorbell, the roar of the lawn mower—they all seem to scream, "She's really just working from *home!*" And then there are the top notes added by children. I picked up the phone to make a call a while back and found that Alex was already on the line—talking to a very surprised Christine Todd Whitman, whom I was profiling for a magazine article. Of course, it could have been worse. A friend's son once beat her to a call from an important client and told him: "Mommy's downstairs, and I'm on the potty so I can't go get her."

The client took it surprisingly well. So did the (then) governor, and we went on to have a charming conversation about her own children. Jocko Lloyd has had success with his new open-door policy, too. He's had one negative reaction—a caller who bristled when he put her on hold to check on a crying child—but it didn't lead him to close his door. Instead, he decided that he and the caller—a potential employer—would not be a good business match.

LIFE'S WORK

WHAT NEXT?

Evan used to walk and talk in his sleep. He would have passionate conversations with us, while clearly completely asleep, and one night, as I steered him back to bed, he announced, "Life is boring. You work and work and work and then you die." I ran for the child psychology books and spent a lot of time talking with him about the joy and fulfillment of work, and how there was more to life than work, but while I did this I secretly thought that the kid wasn't really wrong. I'd had the same realization myself, when I was years older than he, during my freshman year of college. All of high school had been spent polishing myself for the college admissions process, so I was alarmed when it dawned on me that I wasn't done. Good grades would be required for grad school, and more good grades would be needed for a good job, and many long nights would be spent to advance in that job. You work and work and work and then you die.

It is, of course, more complex than that. The more I write about life and work, the more I see that I do not just give myself to my work. My work gives something back to me. At the same time, though, I also see how I rely on work for my identity. I am Mike and Janet's daughter, yes, and Bruce's wife, and Evan and Alex's mom. I'm a decent ice skater, an eager traveler, a voracious reader, a contented baker, a passionate friend, and an encyclopedia of old Broadway show tunes. But I am also very much a writer. So who am I once I'm not that last part anymore?

I find myself asking that a lot lately, of those who are further along this road, and as far as I can tell, you end work in the same spirit in which you began it. My father, who was always content with his work but never consumed by it, retired easily and happily. He is delighted with his new life as a former orthodontist, and his days are so full that he wonders when he ever found the time to straighten teeth. My mother, on the other hand, can't bring herself to retire. She's still changing careers every half a decade or so to keep from getting bored. She says she can't imagine her life without a job to go to. That does not bode well for me.

From my vantage point at the moment—decades closer to retirement than I've ever been but still decades away—I'm beginning to see that this decision may be like so many others I've made along the way. In other words, I'll close my eyes and I'll jump.

Here's to nice soft landings.

BACK FROM LUNCH

Brandon and Jill Lowitz were thin and tan when they returned from their adventure in Bali. They were also full of thoughts about how work looks when you stop doing it, at least for a while. They had lived out our collective fantasy, ditching deadlines and goals, and they were back to report that sometimes a little of each of those things isn't all that bad.

Their first surprise was how easily they could leave the world of work behind. Dinner conversation at their house used to be about her project or his client or the latest skinny on their friends from the office. But in Bali Brandon said, "We put that away almost from day one. We found a slew of other things to talk to each other about." And when they E-mailed those office friends, "I never asked anything about work," he said. "I asked about their families, or what they were doing with their lives, but nothing about what was going on with an account."

This clean break was made easier because they were in a part of the world where work is too scarce and too hard to become anyone's identity. In Indonesia, for instance, they spent days returning again and again to a shop that advertised lessons in batik dyeing but never found anyone around to teach them. "No one cared what we did for a living," Jill said. "We would tell people we'd both stopped working so we could travel, and no one asked what work we had done before. Here it's the first question. There they don't even ask."

But while they did not miss work, and certainly did not miss working in New York City during the heat of the summer, they did miss the structure and contrast that work brings. Going to work defines the day, giving it a beginning and an end. It divides work time from play time, and even though we blur and abuse those lines, we are still steadied by the fact that they are there. "It's strange to wake up in a foreign country and not know what to do for the day, where to eat, what to see, when to see it, and how to get there," Brandon said. "I can honestly say that if we lived in a society without work, there would be a lot of bored people on the street."

To their surprise, they felt unmoored without the small goals and the mini-accomplishments—activities as fleeting but satisfying as checking a task off a to-do list. They found themselves role-playing professions, declaring Jill to be the "professional photographer" for their trip and Brandon the "professional writer." They took these jobs seriously, not wanting to leave a moment of the adventure unrecorded, and Jill discovered a deep creative vein while snapping hundreds of evocative close-ups and dreamy black-and-whites.

Now and again they would catch a glimpse of CNN, so they knew that "the economy back home was heading for the toilet," Brandon said. Nonetheless, they didn't think any "macro thoughts" about their future until they were on the plane back home. "I miss working," Brandon realized when he did allow himself to wonder what he was going to do next. "I miss the interaction with coworkers and clients. Working is part of the game. We must work to live. Work gives structure, it gives routines, and even though we may complain about them, it's okay to have them."

He began his reentry by working part-time as a consultant for his former boss while fleshing out some business ideas of his own about how the Internet can be applied to the travel industry. Jill started looking for a more artistic kind of work than she was doing before—ideally designing a line of shoes or handbags. They are committed to reentering the work world with the same determination with which they left it. It's time to start saving again for a down payment on an apartment, time to resume living a real life.

"This trip was not to 'find ourselves' or discover who we are," Jill said. "It was to give us a window in both our working and personal lives. Having separated ourselves from the grind will keep us going in the future."

CHANGE OF LIFE

Just a few years ago, Dan Gross would have said he had this work-life thing all figured out. Simply put, his work *was* his life. Back in the winter of 1997 he was the youngest partner at the J. Walter Thompson advertising agency, where he earned a lot of money to persuade the rest of us to buy things like Kodak film and Lipton teas. He had just turned thirty, and as he celebrated at a dinner with his family, he remembers growing misty-eyed because his life was so good.

The next afternoon, Dan's younger brother, Matthew, was shot in the head by an armed militant at the top of the Empire State Building. (Matthew survived, but has never really recovered.) Dan learned of the shooting when the Knicks game he was watching (while analyzing the commercials) was interrupted by a news report. Almost immediately, he said, "Selling tea and film and mouthwash didn't seem important anymore." He'd heard of people who anesthetize themselves with work, burying themselves in the office, grateful for the diversion. He tried that, but although he showed up at his job, only his outer shell was there.

Most of the time, our work shapes our lives, leaving us to fit life in around the edges in the spare time that work allows. But sometimes life steps in and takes charge of our work. In a single, shattering moment, the path you planned to travel to retirement becomes one you can't bear to set foot upon again.

Karen Borkowsky's moment came in December of 1998, back when she was a buyer in the shoe department of Macy's, a job that brought her happiness in the form of limitless pairs of shoes. It was consuming work, and she used to joke that the store's slogan "We're a Part of Your Life" should be changed to "We're Your Entire Life," because of the time she gave to the store.

When she was diagnosed with breast cancer at the age of thirty-two, Karen wanted to cling to work. She was back at Macy's shortly after the second of her two mastectomies, and she came in every day while undergoing chemotherapy. Halfway through her treatment she was promoted to director of women's shoes, a job she used to think she wanted. But after four months of slogging in every day, she had a revelation; while her fear had been that she would not be able to work, her problem was that she didn't want to work. "My heart wasn't in it," she said. "Going in and worrying whether my shoes were on the selling floor just didn't do it for me."

What did "do it" for her was walking. She had been an avid runner before her cancer (in fact, she was diagnosed soon after running the New York City Marathon) and during the worst of her chemo she began training for a three-day, sixty-mile Avon-sponsored fund-raising walk against breast cancer, so that she would have a goal. Every morning, "even when I felt sick," she would walk between eight and ten miles and think about what she should do with her life. By the end of the summer she had raised $41,000 in pledges, walked the walk, and quit her job. Soon after that she joined the staff of the American Cancer Society as the organizer of Making Strides Against Breast Cancer, a five-mile fund-raising walk.

Dan Gross, in turn, left his partnership at J. Walter Thompson and went into a different kind of advertising. He is the founder of PAX, a nonprofit group that creates media campaigns against gun violence. You might have seen his wave of billboards and TV spots—informing parents that 40 percent of households have guns and urging them to ask if there is a gun in the house before sending their children to play at a friend's. (Just as an aside, he has certainly convinced me.)

Both Dan and Karen asked me not to turn their lives into Happily Ever Afters—workaholic-sees-the-light-and-takes-a-pay-cut-but-has-never-felt-more-fulfilled. Yes, they said, they do relish going to work in the morning with a sense of purpose. But work that is an expression of a life carries its own burdens. Said Dan: "A side effect of this is that I remind myself, on a daily basis, about the worst thing that ever happened in my life. That can wear at you."

Agreed Karen: "The difference between buying shoes and changing the world is that people used to call me up to ask me about fall styles. Now people call me up to tell me that someone they know has been diagnosed with breast cancer."

HUBIE

Hubert Green—he'd like you to call him Hubie—is eighty-four years old and has been an air-conditioning engineer since the end of World War II. That is longer than he ever thought he would work, certainly longer than anyone around him has worked, and although he has fleeting thoughts of retirement, he does not know how to make a decision that final.

"I would never want to work where I'm not wanted," he said. "I guess I'll just get the message when it's time to go."

We stumble into the workplace through a mixture of instinct, planning, happenstance, and gravitational pull. Then, decades later, we stumble out the same way. Hubie learned his trade in the army, back when air-conditioners were run on sulfur dioxide, not Freon. He is what's known as an "estimator," the math whiz who calculates how to most efficiently cool large commercial buildings. "It's a lot like playing bridge," he said. "You have to use your wits to figure out the best way, the most economical way." He does this today much as he always has, with a slide rule, plain and simple.

"My slide rule," he boasted, "can do things a computer can't."

He tried to hang up that slide rule once, at age sixty-seven, when his boss brought in two sons to learn the trade. A few months later he was back because "I couldn't stand the nothing days." Then the year Hubie turned eighty-three, the same boss hired a "young fellow" as a second estimator, and Hubie tried to quit again. But within a month the new man was gone, and now Hubie "has even more work than I had before."

He wanted it made clear that he is not a windup machine and that time has taken its toll. He cut back to a three-day workweek (which he increases from time to time, so the boss can go on vacation). He also stopped climbing on roofs at project sites, leaving others to report back what they see.

And he hoped he did not sound like an old fogey when he said that "my younger compatriots" don't seem to understand what real work is. "I'm disappointed in the younger people," he said. "I've seen young people out of college multiply fifty by ten and they need a piece of paper. Can't do anything in their head." They also aren't made of his sterner stuff. "They take sick days," he said. "I never take them. I'd feel just as bad staying home as going to work, so I might as well get some work done."

Jordan Lazzari, seventy-seven, has watched the work ethic change, too. He began as an insurance claims adjuster in 1950, and worked at that job until he retired in 1986. Bored, he took on a two-week temporary assignment with an insurance company and then stayed for more than ten years. His grudging concession to age was that he would work only from 7 A.M. to noon. But, said Wayne Nolan, the man who recruited him in the first place, "he does more in those five hours than most other people do all day."

Jordan and Hubie remind me of younger versions of my great-aunt Minnie, the one who was already in her eighties when she began her acting career. Time caught up with Aunt Minnie, and she's had to stop working; the days became too tiring and she couldn't trust her brain to hold on to her lines. Jordan Lazzari finally had to stop, too. He tumbled down a flight of steps on a job one day, breaking more bones than he could count. "I think I've had it," he said. "All I've known is claims, but my bones ache. I think I'm going to pack it in."

Hubie Green predicted he would make his decision the same way. In other words, he will never choose to leave; he will let time decide for him. "Luckily for me, the firm is expanding," he said. "There's plenty for me to do."

SUCCESSION

Jay Newton has four children: Three are sons, and one is a 15,000-square-foot restaurant in Phoenix, Arizona. He opened the sprawling Beef Eaters steak house forty years ago and has given his heart to the place ever since. Even at age eighty-three, he was at work by 8 A.M. and stayed until well after the dinner rush. Of course, his commute was an easy one—he lives in the small matching bungalow that is connected to the restaurant by a small patio.

Jay knew for a while that it was time for someone else to run Beef Eaters. But how to choose that someone? How do you pass along the sweat-stained, love-stoked sum of your life's work? Is success measured by the sale price of the business or by the grace with which you bow out? If you insist on control even after you're gone, does this mean you're irrationally obsessed or justifiably proud?

For years Jay assumed that his children would take over. After all, his oldest son is a kitchen chef, and his middle son owns a local sports bar, meaning both are well prepared to take the helm of the family restaurant. But the chef made it clear that he wants to cook, not manage, and the bar owner had no interest in his father's quaint world of black leather banquettes, thick red carpets, and antique suits of armor. (The youngest of the three had health problems that would keep him from the job.)

The more he thought about it, in fact, the more Jay realized he did not want to give this restaurant to his sons, because, with its round-the-clock responsibilities, the job was too hard. He did not want them to live the life that he has led. "This style of restaurant demands that you almost live in it," he said, explaining why he built his bungalow in the first place. "If I had my life to live over again, I wouldn't go into the restaurant business."

So Beef Eaters will go to strangers, which makes it typical of an American small business. According to Michael Trueblood, director of the Family Business Council, while ninety percent of businesses in the United States are family owned, "only thirty percent are successfully passed to the second generation, and thirteen percent are successfully passed to the third generation."

That said, Jay turned his thoughts to whom the strangers should be. He entertained several prospective buyers, but none of them would promise not to change his restaurant. "The people who have been interested have wanted to make it a Mexican place, or a banquet hall, or part of some chain," he said.

This, too, is typical of small business owners. "The business has values to the owner, which are not business values," said Wes Tyler, founder of Old Oak Partners, a family-business consulting firm. He compared the emotions that grow up around a business to the ones that grow up around a house. "People have refused to sell to buyers who criticize their wallpaper," he said.

After rejecting his logical paths of succession, Jay Newton hit upon a most illogical one. He decided to give Beef Eaters away. He announced an essay contest, and said he would hand the restaurant to the winner. Something like Willy Wonka and his golden tickets, or the "Yo! I'm Your CEO" contest held by Ben & Jerry's in 1994. (No one actually won that contest, by the way. A head-hunting firm found Robert Holland Jr., a former partner at McKinsey & Company, Inc., who was asked to submit an entry anyway before being appointed to the job.)

Soon a new breed of potential owner started showing up for a tour of Beef Eaters. "I can just see it in their eyes," Jay said hopefully. "They have the same feeling about this place as I do."

They also had something else—a hundred-dollar application fee. That's not much to pay for a restaurant, to be sure, but if you read the fine print you'll get an idea of what made Jay such a sharp businessman in the first place. He estimated that the value of Beef Eaters is $2.5 million, and he reserved the right to call off the contest (and refund all application money) if he received fewer than 25,000 applications. He also will retain title to the land on which the building sits, as well as the bungalow that is now his home.

"I worked my whole life for this," he said. "This is a way of leaving without going anywhere. I'll be haunting the new owner for a long time."

WHEN WE GROW UP

Back when he was in kindergarten, Alex announced that he would be a mountain climber when he grew up. But since mountain climbing didn't pay very well, he would support himself with a truly lucrative career—art.

I will never be a mountain climber or an artist. I will never sing in front of a shrieking crowd at Wembley Stadium, and I will never hear "The Star Spangled Banner" as I accept a gold medal. Over time, doors close and options dwindle. One day you realize that you are whatever it is you are going to be.

Watching kids play dress-up with professions makes us peer into the full-length mirror, too. In one single reflection we see two things: their futures and our accumulated choices from the past. If we like what we see, should we steer them down whatever road we've taken? If we wish we'd done something different, should we lead them someplace else?

The questions are toughest, of course, when we carry regret or second guesses, when we find ourselves hoping that our children don't do what we do or become what we are. Peter Cimbolic, the dean of graduate studies at Catholic University of America in Washington, is a psychology professor who also sees private patients. Several years ago his daughter, Katie, nervously admitted that she was applying to graduate school in psychology.

Peter tried to talk his daughter out of his footsteps. He told her that the field of psychology was overcrowded, that academic jobs were impossible to find, and that private practice was even more frustrating because insurance rules make it hard to earn a living. "With your academic credentials, you can do anything," he told her. She answered: "I love doing this."

Then there are the moments when, with a rush of pride and a tinge of envy, you realize your children have talents for your line of work that you have never had. Robert Villency took over the Maurice Villency furniture company from his father in the early 1960s, after the older man's appendix burst. The business was just one small store in Greenwich Village back then. On Robert's watch it grew dramatically, but not because he had a feel for furniture. "I don't have many aesthetic bones in my body," he said.

His son, Eric, does. "Eric has my father's design sense and sense of fashion," said Robert Villency. Eric joined the company three years ago, at age twenty-two, and before coming on board he told his father, "I want to be able to change things. As far as I'm concerned, nothing is sacred design-wise." Then he brought in a new chief designer and new advertising staff. "It's Eric who's going to take this company to the next level," his father said.

As parents, we dream that our children will go further

than we ever will. But it can be bittersweet to watch that dream come true, to see them smack-dab at the beginning of their adventure, knowing we are ever closer to the end. Cherie Kerr is a writer and performer who was in the original troupe of Groundlings. She is the founder of a spin-off group called the Orange County Crazies, and she has brought her son, Drake Doremus, to rehearsals since he was four years old. He caught the bug. For ten years he has had a part in every Crazies show, and as a teenager he took an office at her theater and opened four original plays.

Drake wrote constantly and could not wait to graduate from high school so he could write full-time. His mother would love to write constantly, but she had to pay the rent, so she interrupted her creative work for stints in public relations or corporate consulting. "His passion is a slap in the head to me," she said. "It's like he's saying, 'Well, I'm doing mine, when are you going to do yours?' There's no stopping this kid," she added. "He's going places I'm not going to go."

When it comes to my own choices, and my own children, I am fighting the urge to give any advice, reminding myself that I would probably be wrong no matter what I say. When I was in high school my mother refused to allow me to learn to type, because the hard-learned lesson of her own life was that typing would limit me to the secretarial pool. She could not have prepared me for the age of computers. What, then, can I not prepare my children for?

Alex, in the meantime, has become a second-grader, wiser and more practical than before. Being a mountain climber is not a job, he says, it's a sport. Now he wants to be a "world traveler" when he grows up. Wherever he travels, I wish him joy. And I hope he lets me tag along.

TIME

Birthdays do not make me feel nearly as old as I feel come New Year's Eve. I think it's the communal countdown in the final seconds, then weeks of miswriting the date on checks because I'm still living in the past, that make me acutely aware of the passage of time. I've had 365 days, my psyche trills. Where did they all go?

Back in college—back when I *thought* I was busy—I spent some spare time reading the playwright Ionesco. "We haven't the time to take our time," he wrote, and I copied that down and tacked it to my bulletin board, my justification for sloppy work and rash decisions. Of course, I now know that I couldn't have been all that busy, because I had spare time to spend on Ionesco.

Then I graduated and began my first job. Talk about busy. In those early years I came to the newsroom early, left late, skipped vacation, and stopped in for at least a few hours most weekends. But my mental scrapbook also contains snapshots of brunch. And hours spent reading the whole of the Sunday paper. After I got married, I shared those brunches and that paper with my husband—before each of us headed off for a few weekend hours of work.

It was not until I had children that I understood what busy was. Bruce and I had never fought during our first four years together, but when Evan was born I found myself picking fights about the one thing I'd always taken for granted. No, not sleep. Time. "The devourer of all things" was how Ovid described it (yes, I'd once had time to read him, too), and now the lack of time was threatening to devour me.

The nadir came one afternoon when I drew up an elaborate chart, with separate columns for the amount of time, down to the minute, that we had each spent alone, together, working, playing, and caring for the baby over the weekend. That it didn't prove the dramatic imbalance I'd set out to prove only fueled my rage even more. I maturely ripped the chart to pieces, tossed it all at my husband, and stormed out of the room.

Life (and time) being relative (no, I never read Einstein), there are people who would see it as a luxury to have time to make a chart in the first place, and even more of a luxury to have a partner at whom they could throw it. "As a single parent," said Jennifer McGregor, who runs a Manhattan consulting company that specializes in public art projects, "I'm dependent on complex, fragile arrangements that include an excellent after-school program, the health of my two girls, the availability of my parents, who live two hundred fifty miles away, and the goodwill of the children's father." Sometimes, she said, the house of cards tumbles, like the day she was at a meeting in Philadelphia and realized she had forgotten to leave a key for the baby-sitter who was picking up the children from a friend's house and bringing them home.

Barbara Laing, in turn, was a professional photographer in Midland, Texas, until her divorce. She loved her job, not only for its creativity but for its flexibility. Every year, she'd hold an elaborate Christmas party, where dozens of neighborhood children would bake and ice hundreds of cookies, then deliver them to area homeless shelters. She would also create a masterpiece of a Christmas card. Once she rented a trampoline and placed it against the backdrop of a cloud-filled sky so she could photograph her children looking as if they were flying.

But with the divorce came a new job—one with fifty-hour workweeks, benefits, and a steady paycheck. There were no cookie parties that year, and no Christmas cards, not even store-bought ones. "It's an acknowledgment that I have limits and can only do so many things," she said. "I just ran out of time," she added, then started to cry.

RESOLUTIONS

I love opening my E-mail on the mornings when the Life's Work column appears. Soon my mailbox is crammed with scores of messages, forming an electric, never-ending conversation about the constant collision of life and work.

The problem is, this conversation takes place inside my computer. It really belongs where it began—out in the world with all of you. So at the end of each year I send an E-mail back to everyone I've heard from asking them to help write a New Year's column. One year the question was: "What are you absolutely, no question, definitely determined to do next year (maybe, if you have time) to make your days less frantic?" In other words, what New Year's resolutions are you making to better handle your work and your life?

Nearly all of the answers had to do with time—specifically making time for more than work. Steven Scalici, who has a new appreciation of time since his fight against prostate cancer, vowed not to "race off the Staten Island ferry" on his way to his Manhattan job as a transportation engineer, but rather to "saunter off like a laggard." He also planned to stop taping television programs that he then has to make time to watch. "If I miss it," he said, "it doesn't get watched."

Todd Ellis Kessler, a television writer in Los Angeles, also vowed to start being "*less* efficient with my time. I fill up so many unoccupied moments with preoccupying thoughts— to-do lists, ideas for scripts, investment plans—that I fail to live the moment itself. So next year, when I'm just sitting at a red light, I plan to do just that and nothing but that."

Beth Haessig, a school psychologist, planned to "have coffee with a friend once a week," and "listen to music once a day." Yvette Durant, an executive secretary, planned to keep the same overloaded schedule but stop complaining about it. "Complaining makes me frantic," she said, "not my schedule." And Bonni Brodnick, who works in media relations, swore that "on the days I am working in my home office, I will meet my ten-year-old daughter at three-thirty at the bus at the end of our road. Very shortly, she will be 'too cool' to want Mommy to meet her at the bus after school."

A remarkable number of you were fiercely determined to earn less. "My resolution," said Avi Weiss, a manager of platform interoperability for OpenWave, "is to spend more time doing what makes me feel good about myself, rather than doing what gets me the most amount of money. I make all this money, but I have to spend too much of my time doing things I don't enjoy or value that I'm not sure I see the point anymore."

And you were equally determined to buy less. "This past year I successfully resisted others' pressure to get a cell phone or even Call Waiting," said Steven L. Rosenhaus, a composer, lyricist, and performer. "I find that these items of 'convenience' are anything but that—making one available at any time, anywhere, whether it's warranted or not. I will not get those items/services in next year either."

Agreed Diane Roback, a senior editor at *Publishers Weekly* magazine: "I am *not upgrading*. Which means, though I do have a cell phone, I don't want to be able to access the Internet on it, and will keep my basic phone. I have a PalmPilot, but I don't want to get my E-mail or the Internet on it. I'm going to try to get away with as minimal technology (without becoming a Luddite) that I can get away with. So I resolve to log out on Fridays and log back in on Mondays, and the world will not come to an end!!"

Many warned that I shouldn't make resolutions at all. Carol Weston was one. "For years," she said, "my New Year's resolution was 'Write a Novel.' I never managed it and I got tired of setting myself up for disappointment, so one year I resolved simply to 'Have Fun.' That was a fun year. It was also the year I wrote a novel."

My favorite resolution (though, in light of Carol Weston's advice, not one I will actually make myself) came from Bonnie Russell, a computer consultant in Silicon Valley. "In an effort to break free from my computer and phone," she said, "I will at least stand while speaking on the phone *and* use free weights to work out my triceps while I talk."

SEPTEMBER 11, 2001

Are we going to remember this time around? Are we going to cling to the lessons we learned that ashen Tuesday? We have vowed to do better before. We have faced tragedy and sworn to hug our children closer, call our parents more often, stop and smell the roses. And for a short while we actually have.

Writing about life and work means flirting with hypocrisy. Every week I chronicle the fight to keep an eye on what's important. In the choice between life and work, I say choose life. Yet getting those eight hundred words onto the page often means losing sight of all I preach. It means putting off my children or feeding my ulcer, because, for the moments I am writing, the writing is the all-enveloping thing. I work because I love it and because I like the goodies it brings me and because it layers order over my life. But on that one awful day I watched live on my office television as the world's most visible workplace disintegrated into rubble. Work cannot bring order in a world of chaos.

No work was done that day. Not around the obliterated

World Trade Center and not anywhere in the country. Our phones didn't work, and our planes didn't fly, and our overnight packages didn't arrive, and it didn't matter. The only job worth doing was rescue work, and the rest of us just sat and watched. We clustered around our television sets, as we did when the *Challenger* exploded, and when the Oklahoma City federal building was bombed, and when shots rang out at Columbine. We didn't bother to cancel meetings, we just assumed they would not happen. We didn't return telephone calls unless they were from someone we love.

It was all about those phone calls. The stock market stopped trading—yet our world went on. The schools let out early, political primaries were postponed, bridges and tunnels were closed—still our world kept spinning. But if there was no answer at the other end of our phone call, if the cell phone of a loved one rang and rang, then our world was frozen, paralyzed in time until we heard their voice.

I carry a list in my wallet, tucked in with the photos of my children, my husband, and my dog. On it are the one hundred sixty-eight names of the victims of the Oklahoma City bombing, and it is there to remind me that life can change in an instant. I was a better human being for a time after that bombing. The spring air sparkled for me, and I lingered with the boys at bedtime just because I could. I hadn't taken the yellowed paper out into the light for months now. Not until that Tuesday morning.

I put it by the phone and I started to call. I couldn't find my parents, and I was frantic until they arrived at my door sobbing because they had not been able to get through to me. My ten-year-old son called from school to make sure I was safe. My husband called from work at the hospital to say he probably would not be coming home for a long time. Even here in Westchester County—forty miles north of Ground Zero—you could hear the sirens, racing south to the scene. I sat down at the computer, not to write but to E-mail. Work was unthinkable. Only the contact mattered.

I often wonder what I would regret should I suddenly get a dreaded diagnosis. That Tuesday, for the first time, I wondered what I would regret if the world should end. As the days that followed brought scenes of Armageddon, the thought began to dawn that I would not change anything about my life. I would just appreciate its every detail more. I wouldn't wish that I had sailed the world or written the great American novel. But I would regret the times I had not marveled at the sheer luxury of normality.

When the towers fell, there were papers everywhere. Millions of sheets, representing thousands of work hours, all blowing aimlessly in the breeze. Those documents were all vitally important at 8:45 that Tuesday morning. Within hours they were nothing but ghostly debris.

I found it hard to work in the days and weeks that followed. I couldn't concentrate worth a damn, the tears flowed when I tried, and any words I wrote seemed trivial against the enormity of the whole. Even then I knew the paralysis would pass, that I would get back to work soon, and that I would keep perspective for a while, then lose it bit by bit. But I vowed to fight with all that's in me to never lose it all. I tucked the list of Oklahoma City victims back in my wallet. And I found a photo of the World Trade Center—before it crumbled—and tacked it on my office wall.

EPILOGUE

Most of the words you just read were written between September 1999 and September 2001. The world has changed since then. I am writing this epilogue as 2001 draws to a close. So much more will change before you read it. And yet I am struck by how much remains the same. We still assume we can do it all, and we are still surprised when we can't. We still beat ourselves up for what we haven't done instead of patting ourselves on the back for all we do.

Some of the people I wrote about in these columns were later caught in the terror of last September. The Reverend Carolyn Yard, for instance, the burn center chaplain, was nearly killed by falling debris from the World Trade Center. Then she picked herself up from the ashes and ran to the nearest hospital, where she ministered to victims for days on end. Dr. Alan Manevitz, the psychiatrist who spoke to me about overstuffed briefcases, spent the night of September 11 at Ground Zero, counseling rescue workers who had lost so many of their own. Steven Scalici, whose New Year's resolution was not to race off the Staten Island ferry, was in a building overlooking the Twin Towers when they fell, and he watched the horror through his office window.

Jane Swift's popularity soared during her three-month maternity leave. Julie Swensen has decided she is better off without her ex, and isn't crying nearly as often. "Having a new boyfriend helps," she says. Jay Newton never found a "buyer" for his restaurant. Only a handful of contestants entered to win Beef Eaters, so he called the whole thing off. He's eighty-four now, and tired of working. "I wouldn't turn down any reasonable offer," he says. Robin Klein lets her husband do the grocery shopping once in a while, though I haven't brought myself to ask Bruce to take charge of the boys' shoes.

Laura Senturia moved to a job with longer hours and more responsibility, and she has not had the time to keep in proper touch with her friend Marybeth. "We E-mail (though not as often as either of us would like)," she says, "and have played phone tag (again, not as often as we should)."

Hubie Green is still working at age eighty-five. He lost his wife of more than fifty years the week that he and I first spoke, and having an office to go to every day, he says, gives his life a focus. Vault.com is still in business, but has changed its name to Vault, Inc., and has had to lay off sixty people, or two-thirds of its staff. Eric Ober no longer works there.

Brandon and Jill Lowitz both found jobs: hers in fashion, his in the Internet. They still try to have lunch when they can, but they aren't placing bets on it anymore. The six months they spent away from work, Brandon says, "have been the best part of our marriage to date. We know each other better and we've both made decisions to not dedicate our life to work so that we can eat at Balthazar or buy this season's Gucci bag. This is not to say we won't work hard— we've always had good work ethics. What we've gained in the last six months is some sort of unexplainable feeling of 'bond' and no dollar amount can buy that."

The *Times* has begun to include boys in their Take Our Children to Work Day, but my boys think that maybe they would rather be at school. Mike Augustyniak won his bet and has kept the weight off. I have not been good about the gym. I started working out with a trainer after I wrote the exercise column, but tore a tendon in my wrist (walking the dog; don't ask) and the whole thing fell apart after that.

Riley is almost housebroken. My office is almost organized. I can easily find everything Sande filed, but there is a growing pile of papers waiting for me to actually do some filing myself.

Flashcom, my DSL provider, never went public. It went bankrupt instead and was taken over by Telocity. Then Northpoint, which maintained the wires connecting me to Telocity, was sold to AT&T, which decided it didn't want to be a middleman in the DSL business anymore. Telocity changed its name to Direct TV DSL. I was eventually reassigned Verizon as my middleman, and now my DSL is working—when it's in the mood.

The summer Barron Lerner and Cathy Seibel took their laptop on vacation, their daughter threw up on it during the drive up to Cape Cod, rendering it useless for the entire two-week trip. Meanwhile, Bruce and I took our laptop to Ireland during the same summer and found that it refused to connect to the Internet for reasons we still don't understand. I think there may be a message in there somewhere.

I still love hotel rooms but hate to fly more than ever. When editing the manuscript for this book I almost took out the chapter about the "Saturday Night Stay," but I left it in and intact for nostalgic reasons. I fervently hope we return to a time when paying too much is our biggest worry when we fly.

My father is still happily retired. My mother just started a new job. I've heard from a remarkable number of strangers named Belkin. None of them seem to be my relatives, but they all have theories about the meaning of our name. My favorite was from Philip J. Belkin, who remembers an elementary school teacher whose hobby was the derivation of last names. She told him that Belkin was originally Belkind. The first half, "belle" or "bela," means beautiful, and "kind" means child. This makes a Belkin a "beautiful child."

My boys stare back from a picture frame as I write this.

Yep. It fits.

ACKNOWLEDGMENTS

Without Alison Cowan and Glenn Kramon there would be no Life's Work column. Glenn is the editor of the Business section, and Alison was his deputy back when they first came up with this idea and decided to trust me with it. I can't thank them enough. Same goes for Brent Bowers, Mickey Meece, Kris Wells, and Joan O'Neill, who deftly edited the Workplace page in *The New York Times* and who have saved me from some very embarrassing mistakes.

I've always said no one would stop to read the column if not for the delightful drawings at the top by Randy Enos. Thanks also to Michaela Williams and Dennis Stern, who smoothed the way; to Katherine Bouton and Adam Moss, for bringing out the best in me; and to countless friends and colleagues at the *Times,* who make me so proud to work there, especially during this past tumultuous year.

Without David Rosenthal there would be no Life's Work book. He called one day and said "This *has* to happen," and so it did. Ditto for Barney Karpfinger, an extraordinary agent and a caring friend, and Amanda Murray, a most graceful ed-

itor, who "got it" from day one. And while we've never met,
I owe a lot to Patty Romanowski Bashe, who polished as she
copy edited, and Elisha Cooper, who drew the adorable
sketches throughout this book. There is nothing so rare as a
writer who loves her editing and her book jacket, and I am
thrilled to be among the happy few.

I don't have room to thank all the strangers who gave me
glimpses of their lives and let me share them with the world,
people who I found through iVillage, ParentSoup, Profnet,
and countless other sites. Thanks especially to all of you who
took the time to write to me first.

All over Westchester County there are small cafés and
bookshops whose managers probably wonder about that
strange woman with the laptop who moved in for hours at a
time. Thank you, Starbucks, Barnes & Noble, City Limits,
Sushi Man, the Silver Tips Tea Room, and especially the
crowd at Cafe Latte.

My friends keep me going, and the nicest thing about
writing a book is that I get to thank them in print for being
my friends. I live in a world filled with Al and Cathy Cattabi-
ani, Bob and Amy Sommer, Todd Kessler and Sharon Hall,
Barron Lerner and Cathy Seibel, Eugene and Jill Hertz,
Mimi Swartz and John Wilburn (thanks, guys, for the book's
title), Barbara Laing, Debra Karl, Doreen Weisenhaus, Bonnie Rothman Morris, David Sanger and Sherill Leonard,
Lisa Wolfe and Joe Ravitch, Nick Kristof and Sheryl Wu
Dunn, Sam and Lisa Verhovek, all the women in my book
club, all the regulars on the annual Turkey Walk, and the
yearly New Year's gang. It's a wonderful place to live.

My debt to my parents is obvious on every page of this
book. They believed in me, encouraged me, and put up with

me. Less obvious, but just as deep, are the thanks owed my brother and sister, the doctors Gary Belkin and Kira Belkin, who were along on this ride from the start. Noemi and Allen Gelb, Dana Gelb Safran and Alan Paul Safran, Masha Schiller Belkin and Saul Fishman joined my family circle more recently but became some of its shiniest links. Without them there would be no Alison, Annie, Michael, Emma, Caroline, or Talia, and the world would be missing a treat.

No, I will not be one of those writers who thanks her dog, but he knows that I care.

Last on the list, because they are the most important of all, are Bruce and Evan and Alex. They are the reason for everything. Without them my life would not work.

ABOUT THE AUTHOR

Lisa Belkin is a reporter for *The New York Times* and author of that paper's Life's Work column about the intersection—or, more accurately, the collision—of life and work. While with the *Times* she has covered everything from the state of Texas to the state of health care. She is the author of *First, Do No Harm*, about a year at a Texas hospital as seen through the prism of its ethics committee, and *Show Me a Hero*, about the effects of a judge's desegregation order on one small neighborhood. Her own personal balancing act includes her husband, Bruce, her young sons, Evan and Alex, and her dog, Riley.